Questions You *Always* Wanted to *Ask*

Swami Mukundananda is a world-renowned spiritual teacher from India, an international authority on mind management, and a bestselling author. He earned his degrees from the prestigious IIT Delhi and IIM Calcutta. He worked with a multinational firm for a short while, then renounced a promising career to enter monkhood. He studied the Vedic scriptures at the feet of Jagadguru Kripaluji Maharaj. For almost four decades now, he has been sharing his vast knowledge through his books, lectures, and life-transformation lectures.

Every day, Swamiji meets hundreds, and even thousands, of people from all walks of life. His steadfast positivity exudes hope, clarity, and a sense of purpose to those who connect with him. He has deeply affected the lives of millions of people who have been drawn by his profound integrity, charismatic personality, and passion to serve. Despite his hectic schedule, those who encounter him experience his warmth and compassion and feel deeply touched by him. Swamiji's lectures are humorous, his arguments are logical and well-laid out, and most of all, his advice is practical. His lectures on social media platforms are loved and followed by millions. Swamiji divides his time between India and the US.

swamimukundananda.org
facebook.com/Swami.Mukundananda
instagram.com/Swami_Mukundananda
twitter.com/Sw_Mukundananda
youtube.com/c/swamimukundananda
linkedin.com/in/swamimukundananda

Other Books by the Author

7 Divine Laws to Awaken Your Best Self
(Also available in Hindi)

7 Mindsets for Success, Happiness and Fulfilment
(Also available in Hindi, Gujarati, Marathi, Oriya & Telugu)

Bhagavad Gita, The Song of God

Golden Rules for Living Your Best Life

Science of Healthy Diet

Spiritual Dialectics

The Art & Science of Happiness

The Power of Thoughts

The Science of Mind Management
(Also available in Gujarati & Telugu)

Yoga for the Body, Mind & Soul

Books for Children

Essence of Hinduism

Festivals of India

Healthy Body Healthy Mind – Yoga for Children

Inspiring Stories for Children (set of 4 books)

Mahabharat: The Story of Virtue and Dharma

My Best Friend Krishna

My Wisdom Book: Everyday Shlokas, Mantras, Bhajans and More

Ramayan: The Immortal Story of Duty and Devotion

Saints of India

Questions You Always Wanted to Ask

With blessings!
Swami Mukundananda

Swami Mukundananda

RUPA

Published by
Rupa Publications India Pvt. Ltd 2023
7/16 Ansari Road, Daryaganj
New Delhi 110002

Sales Centres
Bengaluru Chennai Hyderabad
Jaipur Kathmandu Kolkata
Mumbai Prayagraj

P-ISBN: 978-93-5702-571-3
E-ISBN: 978-93-5702-572-0

First impression 2023

10 9 8 7 6 5 4 3 2 1

Printed in India

This book is dedicated to my beloved Spiritual Master, Jagadguru Shree Kripaluji Maharaj, the embodiment of divine love and grace, who illuminated humankind with the purest rays of divine knowledge. He was immersed in the highest bliss of divine love and engaged in inundating the entire planet with it. I am eternally indebted to Him for bestowing upon me His divine wisdom and for inspiring me to consecrate my life to its propagation. I pray that by His blessings this book will help sincere seekers gain a deeper understanding of the positive impacts of spirituality and inspire them to integrate it in their daily life.

Contents

Introduction

Humans are curious beings. From a young age itself, we start to question about the world around us. As children, we wonder in amazement about our surroundings and ponder over fun facts. On receiving answers, our thirst is quenched, only to arise again with further inquiries. And in this manner, we keep probing and learning into adulthood.

As we grow, our inquisitiveness takes on a new form—the questions become deeper and more profound. These queries become the heart of discovery in all spheres of our lives. Everyone has their share of questions that are important to them. They seek knowledge and wisdom they believe will unlock new doors and possibilities, eventually leading to a happy and better life.

Right answers lift us to higher levels of understanding and connect us with unexplored opportunities. This is why acquiring knowledge has been exalted in the sacred texts. The Bhagavad Gita explains:

sarvaṁ jñāna-plavenaiva vṛijinaṁ santariṣhyasi

(verse 4.36)

'Seat yourself in the boat of knowledge, and cross over the ocean of life and death.' Such is the power of true wisdom! Even one deep insight has the power to transform our life. It illumines our intellect, which changes our underlying beliefs and thoughts, thereby steering us towards success.

We all search for answers in various ways. While we find some viable explanations, many questions still linger in our minds or even hold us in a gridlock, making us feel stuck. The dialectic process of question and answer provides a perfect medium for resolution. When done with the help of an expert, it not only clears our doubts but also helps us develop new ideas about the world around us.

The journey of self-discovery often leads us to ask the big questions: 'Who am I?', 'What is the purpose of life?', 'What is true happiness?', 'How can we alleviate suffering?', and so forth. The Vedas simplify the search for us. They guide us to seek a spiritual teacher who can edify the way to purposeful and effective living. The holy books state:

tad viddhi praṇipātena pariprashnena sevayā
upadekṣhyanti te jñānaṁ jñāninas tattva-darśhinaḥ

(Bhagavad Gita 4.34)

'Learn the Truth by approaching a Spiritual Master. Inquire from him with reverence and render service unto him. Such an enlightened Saint can impart knowledge unto you because he has seen the Truth.'

Finding a bona fide Spiritual Master is a process that requires patience. In the meantime, what do we do about our questions? The answer is simple. Search for answers but in the right places.

And for those who have found their Guru, it is not always feasible to access them personally for every doubt that arises in the mind. The alternative, again, is to refer to an impeccable source of knowledge.

For all ardent seekers of insightful answers, the book in your hands gives you easy access to wisdom that would otherwise be gained by sifting through endless piles of information and wading through much confusion. In this book, you will obtain guidance on questions related to spirituality, philosophy, mind management, devotion, life's dilemmas, professional mastery, self-transformation, and more.

Questions like 'Why do good people suffer?', 'What is the secret to mental strength?', 'What is the role of destiny?', 'How should I meditate?', 'How should I practise spirituality at home?', 'Which form of God should I worship?', 'How should I deal with insults?', and 'How do I achieve focus at work?', along with a plethora of other relevant issues, have been explained in this ready reference guide.

A sincere effort has been made to explain every subject with sound reasoning and perfect logic. The goal is not just to satisfy your curiosity but to do so in the most convincing manner that leaves no room for conjecture. The answers are validated with relevant quotations from sacred texts, testimonies of other Saints, and personal insights. They are further enhanced with relatable stories, scientific research, and real-life examples.

It is said: 'Seek and you shall find.' The fact that you are reading this book confirms you have questions and are in search of answers. My best wishes to you as you utilize this guidebook to gain a deeper understanding of life, uncover new ideas that will expand your horizons, and acquire wisdom to solve your personal problems and dilemmas. In doing so, may you experience many realizations and epiphanies with every page of this book.

Swami Mukundananda

1

Faith—Good or Bad Thing

BLIND FAITH VS TRUE FAITH

Question: How can we distinguish between 'true faith' and 'blind faith'? How can we avoid becoming followers with blind faith?

Answer: We cannot exist without faith, and it is required at every step of our life. Eating at a restaurant needs faith that the waiter did not poison your food. Getting your beard shaved at the barbershop requires trust that the barber will not slit your throat with his sharp knife. Without a leap of faith, we cannot function.

Scientists look down upon spiritualists for being people of faith. But they do not realize that they, too, work on the premise of faith. They choose to believe the information their senses convey to them. The perception of the senses could be misleading. But the leap of faith must be made, for, without it, the experimental process of science cannot even begin.

In conclusion, **we all live by faith. Where we choose to place it determines the direction of our life.** For example, some believe wealth is of paramount importance, so they spend their entire life accumulating it. Others are convinced fame is the measure of success, and they pursue it passionately in all things. Yet others develop deep faith in the attractiveness of God-realization, and they renounce material pleasures in search of the Supreme.

Faith, thus, determines the values we live by, the choices we make, and the direction our life takes. How does our faith develop? In various ways.

Some beliefs come from the family and environment. For example, people's beliefs about politics are often determined more by family upbringing than by deep analysis. As they say in the US, 'Children of Democrats become Democrats, while children of Republicans become Republicans.' Likewise, people usually do not make a conscious choice about the religion they follow. They are born into a particular tradition and accept it because their parents and grandparents did.

Other beliefs are based on experience. A student makes a couple of attempts at the game of tennis and fails. Impulsively, she assumes she can never be good at sports. She may have done well in other sports, but she develops a conviction about her inabilities.

Some beliefs come from hearsay. This was seen in Germany during the Nazi regime. Hitler and his cohorts duped Germans into believing gross untruths, leading their nation to the Second World War. Hitler's minister, Joseph Goebbels, expressed his tactics: 'If you tell a lie a thousand times, it will become the truth.'

The worst kind of faith is blind faith—which is believing in something unquestioningly or without discrimination, or choosing to trust against evidence and reasoning.

I often come across this type of faith while preaching. There are people who believe the Mahabharat can lead to quarrels in their family, so they are afraid to keep it at home while the truth is the reverse. The Mahabharat is a treasure chest of wisdom and morals that provides the good sense to reduce conflicts. But since the background of the epic is a war setting, these people blindly believe it will create conflict in their home as well.

Many others perform irrational rituals of sacrificing animals to goddesses simply because their ancestors did so. They do not question why. The same applies to superstitions. Black cats are considered bad luck, while keeping a horseshoe apparently wards off evil.

Blind faith can be extremely dangerous. It results in incorrect attitudes, bad choices, and adverse actions. In modern times, social media makes it easier to form false beliefs through fake news, which many people, unfortunately, take for real. Our goal is to form good beliefs in order to take our life in the proper direction. So, how can we develop faith that is auspicious and true?

The basis of good beliefs is correct knowledge. Saint Tulsidas states in the Ramayan:

jāneṅ binu na hoi paratītī, binu paratīti hoi nahiṅ prītī

'Without true knowledge, there cannot be true faith; without true faith, there cannot be true love.' Thus, knowledge has a pivotal role to play in the journey of life. The Bhagavad Gita states:

na hi jñānena sadṛiśhampavitramiha vidyate (verse 4.38)

'There is nothing as purifying as divine knowledge.' So, make good knowledge the basis of your beliefs. This naturally leads us to the next question.

FAITH IN THE SCRIPTURES AND THE GURU

Question: What is the right way to gather spiritual knowledge? Why should we have faith in the scriptures?

Answer: Good beliefs are formed based on trustworthy and reliable knowledge. Such knowledge is free from the imperfections of the human intellect. Where can we find such knowledge?

There are three sources for divine wisdom: 1) Vedic scriptures, 2) writings of Saints, and 3) the Guru. Let us understand this a little better.

The Vedas. These holy books are called *apauruṣheya*, meaning, not created by humans. They were manifested by God Himself at the beginning of creation in the heart of the firstborn Brahma. They were passed down by oral tradition. At the beginning of Kali yug, Ved Vyas put them down in writing and divided them into four parts. However, the Vedas existed even before him.

In Hindu philosophy, the Vedas are accorded the highest place because they contain knowledge from a perfect source.

bhūtaṁ bhavyaṁ bhaviṣhyaṁ cha sarvaṁ vedāt prasidhyati

(*Manu Smṛiti* 12.97)

'The veracity of any spiritual principle—past, present or future—is established on the authority of the Vedas.' A section of these Vedas is the Upanishads, which have been extolled by Eastern and Western scholars alike.

The Vedic knowledge has been further elaborated in other scriptures. These include the two *Itihās* (Ramayan and Mahabharat), 18 Puranas, *Shad Darshan* (six treatises on philosophy), 100 *Smritis* (books of dharma), and thousands of *Nibandhs* (philosophical theses by great sages). Together, this entire body of literature is referred to as the Vedic scriptures. These sacred books are full of wisdom.

The Guru. The knowledge in the scriptures is so sublime that it is not easy to comprehend on our own. Their complexities can easily baffle an unguided reader. Hence, the Vedas themselves instruct that they should be understood under the guidance of a Guru. *āchāryavān puruṣho veda* (*Chhāndogya Upanishad* 6.14.2) 'To learn the Vedic scriptures, approach a Spiritual Master.'

In modern times, fortunately or unfortunately, we have access to numerous gurus who present many contrasting ideas and methodologies. How do we know which guru's interpretation is correct? Is there any way to validate whether a guru is teaching the Absolute Truth and not just sharing his personal opinion? Fortunately for us, there is.

The veracity of the Guru's teaching can be validated in two ways:

1) **It should align with the wisdom of the scriptures.** If not, then it will cause one to doubt that the knowledge he bestows could just be his personal viewpoint and therefore erroneous. Even if one per cent of knowledge is fallacious, it becomes unreliable. In case you are not familiar with the topics related to your Guru's teachings, you can always research more and see if it aligns with the scriptures.
2) **It should be in accordance with the teachings of past Gurus.** The Absolute Truth is not something new to be discovered. It has always existed, and innumerable Saints in the past have taught the way to it. There have been many Gurus in Indian history, such as Soordas, Tulsidas, Meerabai, Kabirdas, Narsi Mehta, Shankaracharya, Madhvacharya, Ramanujacharya, Nimbarkacharya, Chaitanya Mahaprabhu and Vallabhacharya. The basic principles of our Guru's teachings should concur with the teachings of previous Gurus.

This is the triad of Guru (our Spiritual Master), Saints (all the other Gurus in history), and Shastras (the Vedic scriptures). When all three—Guru, Saints, and Shastras—confirm the same principle, then we can safely conclude our Guru is teaching the Absolute Truth. At that point, we must surrender our intellect to him and develop true faith. This is complete faith that is reposed in a perfect source of knowledge.

Why is complete faith necessary? Many times, with our limited intellect, we are unable to comprehend the profound advice of the Guru. However, we must not let that stop us from believing. We must accept even perplexing teachings and apply ourselves to sadhana. Later, as we progress on the path, their veracity will become evident. The *Śhwetāśhvatar Upanishad* states:

yasya deve parā bhaktiryathā deve tathā gurau
tasyaite kathitā hyarthāḥ prakāśhante mahātmanaḥ

(mantra 6.23)

'The import of all Vedic knowledge is revealed within the hearts of those who engage in devotion with unflinching faith in Guru and God.' This is the power of true faith in the Guru.

A story of Sananda, a disciple of Adi Shankaracharya, illustrates this.

Sananda was illiterate and could not comprehend his Guru's teaching like the other disciples. But when Shankaracharya taught, he would listen with rapt attention. One day, Sananda was washing his Guru's clothes on the other side of a river. It was time for class, and all the other disciples requested, 'Guruji, please begin.'

Shankaracharya replied, 'Let us wait. Sananda is not yet here.'

'But Guruji, he cannot understand anything,' the disciples urged.

'That is true, but he listens with great faith,' said Shankaracharya. 'I do not wish to disappoint him.' Then, to show the power of faith, Shankaracharya called out, 'Sananda! Please come here.'

On hearing his Guru's words, Sananda did not hesitate a moment. Without further thought, he ran on water. Wherever he placed his feet, lotus flowers sprang up from the water below to support him. He crossed over to the other bank and offered obeisance to his Guru. He then delivered a stuti *(verses in praise) of his Guru in sophisticated Sanskrit. The other disciples were amazed to hear him.*

Subsequently, Sananda became known as 'Padmapada', or 'the one under whose feet lotuses bloomed'. He was one of the four chief disciples of Shankaracharya. He was the first head of the Govardhan Peeth in Puri.

The story demonstrates the power of true faith. It is 'true' because it is reposed in the right place—in scriptures and Guru. Such faith has the power to radically transform us.

FAITH IN OUR ABILITY TO SUCCEED

Question: After repeatedly failing to achieve goals in life, I now feel like a failure and have lost belief in myself. How can I regain my shattered self-confidence?

Answer: If we believe we cannot succeed, it will become a self-fulfilling prophecy. Thus, bad beliefs are our foremost enemies. Ironically, they reside within our own subconscious mind but render us ineffective in facing external challenges. Franklin Roosevelt, the legendary US president, very aptly said: 'Men are not prisoners of fate, but only prisoners of their own minds.'

This simple story demonstrates the impact of false convictions.

A merchant, travelling with his three camels, stopped at an inn for the night. He began tying his camels to pegs outside the tavern. However, after tying two camels, he fell short of rope for securing the third one. He got a brilliant idea. He simply pretended to put a noose around the camel's neck, and then attach it to a peg. Thinking it was tied, the third camel sat down timidly, like the others.

In the morning, when he was ready to leave, the merchant untied the ropes of the first two camels. They got up and were ready to walk. However, the third camel refused to budge. The merchant could not figure out the reason for its obstinacy. Then he realized that the camel still believed it was tied. So, the merchant pretended to untie the rope. In a moment, the third camel also stood up and joined the other two.

Like the camel, many times, we involuntarily tie ourselves to false beliefs. Though we do not realize it, these self-made chains limit us from achieving our highest potential. We must, therefore, meticulously dismantle debilitating beliefs, such as 'My future is gloomy', 'Success is not possible for me', and 'I am a failure'.

To vanquish such false ideas, use the power of knowledge to illuminate and dispel them. This can be done in any of the following ways:

1) **Remind yourself that you are not the material body.** Develop faith in the splendour of your soul, which is eternal, immortal, and imperishable. Instead, if you think of yourself as merely a bag of flesh and bones, it will cripple your estimation of your potential.

2) **Remind yourself that you are a fragment of the Almighty.** Hence, you possess immense capability. Compare this to a huge fire and its tiny spark. The forest fire can incinerate an entire woodland. The teeny-weeny glow, in comparison, appears minuscule, but it can also bring down the whole

forest. Likewise, the Law of Infinite Potential states: 'All souls have infinite potential for growth, irrespective of their present state.' (*7 Divine Laws to Awaken Your Best Self*)

3) **Your Divine Father has a great destiny in store for you.** This is the reason why He created you. Having faith in His benevolence will lead you to believe in infinite possibilities for personal growth.

At present, we are manifesting only a fraction of our potential. Medical science informs us that the human brain has 100 billion neurons, with scope for trillions of circuits amongst them. We use only 4 per cent of our mental capacity. Imagine what we would achieve if we could unlock our entire potential!

Take inspiration from people who seemed like failures in early life, but eventually, succeeded in a big way.

Mary Kom grew up in a poor family in the northeastern state of Manipur. As a child, she helped her parents with farm chores. She changed many schools purely for financial reasons. But with sheer hard work and determination, she became the only woman boxer in history to win the World Amateur Boxing Championship six times.

Abdul Kalam was rejected by the Indian Air Force, shattering his dreams of becoming a pilot. Yet, he went on to shine as a scientist at Defence Research and Development Organisation (DRDO) and Indian Space Research Organisation (ISRO). Even there, he failed multiple times in the process of developing satellites and warheads. But the 'Missile Man of India' persevered and finally put India in the elite group of six nations holding rare satellite and missile technology.

Narendra Modi used to sell tea for a living but rose to become the prime minister of the largest democracy in the world, with one-sixth of the world population.

Abraham Lincoln failed numerous times in business and politics, before getting elected as the sixteenth President of the United States at the age of 52.

Mahatma Gandhi set up a law practice in Mumbai. However, during his first courtroom case, he was so nervous that he could not cross-examine the witness. Embarrassed, he reimbursed his client for his legal fees. But he did not give up on his life. He went on to lead India's freedom struggle.

All these world-famous people had their pathways strewn with obstacles. What differentiated them from failures? It was their belief that success was possible if only they worked hard enough and smart enough. If they had allowed disappointments to shatter their faith, they would not have created footprints in the sands of time.

So, believe in your potential to achieve great things. You will then be enthused to choose high goals in life. Even though success may not presently be visible on the horizon, keep working towards it. And remember, in the process, at the very least, you are becoming a better person and getting closer to the perfection destined for you.

2

Self-Mastery Skills

TECHNIQUE OF VISUALIZATION

Question: Personality development coaches emphasize the technique of visualization. Why is it considered so powerful, and what is the right way to do it?

Answer: Visualization is a technique that high achievers and world-class athletes use for peak performance. With its help, they mentally practise and fine-tune their subconscious to lift their skills to superhuman levels.

The technique is not rocket science; we all can do it. In fact, we already visualize many times a day. The problem is that we picturize fruitless things—present failures, past regrets, and future worries. Hence, rather than working to our benefit, this powerful tool adversely affects our state of mind.

What is visualization? It is a mental rehearsal of a future performance. It could also be the picturization of what we cherish to be. In it, you create images of what you wish to do or how you desire to become. You mentally engage all your sense perceptions—sight, smell, touch, taste, and sound—to make it as vivid as possible. And then repeat these images again and again for a few minutes every day, until they get embedded in your subconscious.

Why is visualization effective? The principle is simple: things are created twice. First, we conceive them in the workshop of our mind. Second, we perform physical actions to manifest them in reality.

For example, if you wish to become a good sitar player, do not limit yourself to physical practice alone. Alongside, envision yourself sitting in front of an elegant sitar. Mentally watch your fingers stroking the strings with precision and finesse. Imagine yourself playing the most beautiful compositions of distinguished music maestros. Visualize the enchanting sound of music filling the air and the joy it brings with it. See yourself plucking the strings dextrously to create the most harmonious sounds in perfect notes. Picture this repeatedly. Doing so will accentuate your existing sitar practice and empower your subconscious to produce better results.

I would, however, like to add a word of caution here. Some people go overboard with their claims about the power of visualization. They say, 'Simply picture yourself becoming a better sitar player and you will achieve mastery', or 'Just imagine yourself growing rich and you will attract wealth', and so on. This is a mistaken notion—spread by popular self-help books—which fails to acknowledge the need for hard work. Visualization can convince your subconscious that you can become wealthy. But you must also put in the requisite effort to realize your dreams.

Here are some ways in which the practice of mental imagery can be utilized.

Use visualization to bring the mind into focus. Most people fritter away their mind's immense potential with an endless chatter of uncontrolled thoughts. These are more often dominated by negativity than by positivity. Instead, if they tap into the power of mental pictures, their stray thoughts can become focussed on the goal.

Programme your subconscious. The subconscious mind is like a huge memory bank carrying images, experiences, phobias, and other emotions from the past. These subliminal memories influence our conscious thoughts and attitudes.

Interestingly, the subconscious does not reason things out logically. It merely believes what it is told multiple times. If, in our conscious mind, we repeatedly think, 'I am sick...I am sick', the subconscious becomes convinced of it. In this way, it gets programmed by our own self-talk and ideas.

Through the technique of visualization, we take conscious charge of our subconscious mind. Then, our progressively programmed inner mind helps create energizing thoughts and ideas. For instance, if you repeatedly visualize your body in great health, the subconscious mind will be convinced that you are well. It will then direct your physical organs to grow in wellness.

Develop a positive mindset. Most of the time, we do not consciously choose our attitudes and emotions. They arise automatically from our subconscious. So, it is vitally important that it be filled with positivity and hope. This is where visualization can be very helpful. When we are convinced deep down that we can achieve success, the attitude of optimism naturally becomes an integral part of our personality. Likewise, we can internalize other uplifting qualities as well.

Picture the image of God. Visualization yields astonishing results when used in sadhana. Our mind has a natural propensity to get attracted to forms. If we provide it with the attractive and venerable form of God, the mind gets a basis for loving the Supreme. This technique, called 'Roop Dhyan Meditation', was popularized by Jagadguru Shree Kripaluji Maharaj. You can read more about it in the question 'How To Meditate'.

In conclusion, visualization is an amazing tool available to all. But most of us have never utilized it consciously to our benefit. So, begin today by spending 15 minutes every day, visualizing how you wish to be and what you wish to accomplish. Let the imagery sink deep into your subconscious, thereby programming it to become your reliable and trustworthy assistant.

HOW TO OVERCOME ANGER

Question: My question is about anger. When others speak untruths about me or something happens against my liking, I get angry. How can I always control my anger and especially in the spur of the moment?

Answer: Anger is one of the most harmful forces in our inner nature. It is like the fire that destroys everything around while burning itself as well. Anger's destructive nature corrodes relationships. It negatively impacts our physical and mental health. Though we all realize the harm anger causes, many people are unable to control it.

The Vedic scriptures describe anger as a *mānas rog*, or disease of the mind. Its vicious effects are described in the Bhagavad Gita:

krodhād bhavati sammohaḥ sammohāt smṛiti-vibhramaḥ
smṛiti-bhranśhād buddhi-nāśho buddhi-nāśhāt praṇaśhyati

(verse 2.63)

'Anger leads to clouding of judgement. This results in bewilderment of the memory. When the memory is bewildered, the intellect gets destroyed; and when the intellect is destroyed, one is ruined.'

Take the scenario of road rage commonly seen on highways. A speeding driver impatiently honks at the car in front. This infuriates the driver ahead who then deliberately refuses to make way. Soon a perilous match of speeding and swerving ensues, resulting in a serious accident and injuries.

If the slightest provocation—not getting one's way—makes a person spin out of control in fury, it is a serious problem. Here are some tangible steps to control and eradicate anger.

Remember that not everything will be as per your wishes. Every situation can result in two possible outcomes—either we get what we seek or we do not. We must be prepared for both. When we make peace with any outcome, we will not be upset. But if we insist things must happen our way, we will get annoyed.

People may, for example, sometimes say unpleasant things to

you. In a democratic country, everyone has the right to freedom of speech. You cannot control what others say or do. However, you can choose to disassociate yourself from their behaviour and remain peaceful. This is a sign of strength and maturity.

Delay your angry response through anger management strategies. These are simple techniques to gain a handle on your mind in the moment of fury. By postponing your reaction, you will discover it is greatly subdued. For this purpose, you could do any of the following:

- Visualize a happy place. The idea is to divert the mind away from the provocative situation. In the meantime, the left brain will kick in. It will make you think more logically and realize the futility of getting angry.
- Engage in deep breathing. The breath and the mind have a strong connection. When we take deep, slow breaths, the speed of thought reduces as well and the mind calms down.
- Be silent. Clamp down your lips so as to not open your mouth, lest your negative sentiments burst forth in the form of angry words. Ambrose Bierce wittily expressed, 'Speak when you are angry, and you will make the best speech you will ever regret.'

These are simple but potent anger management techniques. When evoked, they buy us time to be more empathetic and reasonable. Practise them to avert a potentially negative response in the heat of the moment.

Bear in mind that to always have control over anger, you must eradicate its root cause. The holy books tell us that anger does not appear randomly. It arises when we want something intensely, and its fulfilment is obstructed. The sense of entitlement and the need to always get desired outcomes land us in trouble. So, desire is the mother of anger.

Give up desires to avoid anger forever. This is the ultimate anger management strategy. If desires go away, anger will also disappear. But would becoming desireless mean we do not seek any happiness? No. The solution is to seek happiness in beneficial things—to dovetail our desires in the direction of the Divine. The Bhagavatam states:

viṣhayān dhyāyataśh chittaṁ viṣhayeṣhu viṣhajjate
mām anusmarataśh chittaṁ mayy eva pravilīyate (11.14.27)

'You repeatedly thought of the pleasures in the objects of the senses and became attached to them. Now, frequently think that God is the Ocean of infinite bliss, and you will develop devotion for Him.'

By contemplating happiness in God, we will develop beneficial desires, such as the aspiration to serve and the thirst for divine wisdom. Unlike material desires, these will purify the mind since the object of attachment is pure. As purity develops, the mind will be less prone to anger. Finally, the day will arrive when we will be totally free from material desires, and then anger will be eradicated from its root.

SECRET OF MENTAL STRENGTH

Question: What is the secret of mentally strong people?

Answer: Mental strength is the toughness to persevere towards our long-term goals, regardless of the challenges on the path. It is also called 'grit', which is unyielding courage in the face of adversity.

Grittier individuals often reach strikingly higher levels of achievement than those with talent, opportunity, and intellect. Mere talent does not suffice in manifesting your latent potential. It must be accompanied by the inner strength to endure until the goal is reached.

The story of former Indian cricketer Yuvraj Singh is a shining example of grit. Yuvraj experienced extraordinary highs and abysmal lows in his career. Fans have cherished him through every moment of his journey, which exuded perseverance, resilience, and passion.

His fascinating career rose to a peak in 2011, when he helped India win the World Cup. For his contribution to the Indian team, he won the 'Man of the Tournament' award. Along the way, he smashed six consecutive sixes in one over.

Almost immediately, his life took a downturn, and he was diagnosed with a malignant tumour. Unfazed, he courageously battled the cancer and recovered from it. Finally, Yuvraj made a triumphant return to the Indian national team. In the history of sports, there are only a few examples of players returning to prominence after beating this disease.

Later, it was revealed that during the 2011 World Cup, he was combating severe symptoms of cancer, which included vomiting blood. Look at his amazing grit. Every time life knocked him down, he displayed the mental toughness to bounce back!

All of us already possess grit, to a lesser or greater extent. To earn your educational degree, you persevered for years. To complete an important project, you stayed up all night. To maintain your job, you bore with its ups and downs. These were all instances where, despite the travails, you persisted on an arduous journey and reached your goal. Now, realizing its importance, practise making it exponentially stronger. How?

Here are some useful tools and techniques for becoming grittier.

Choose to be persistent. Most people give up too soon—sometimes even when they are close to reaching their goal. They lack the tenacity to continue in the face of failure. But those who succeed do so by surmounting the obstacles without quitting.

Overnight success is a rarity, and success without failure, is even more so. Those who are experts today also started off as novices. They practised their craft over and over again, without being discouraged. So, firmly resolve that persistence is necessary for accomplishing your worthy goals.

Build resilience. This is the ability to bounce back after repeatedly being knocked down. Think of persistence as the engine that propels you towards your goal, while resilience is the oil that keeps the engine moving.

Take inspiration from gold. It withstands a thousand blows without breaking, while mud pots get smashed on the first strike.

Align with a higher purpose. Studies have revealed that individuals motivated by an objective beyond themselves have greater inner courage. It is the difference between building a house for yourself and building a temple for God. With a higher purpose, your intellect thinks of several reasons for not giving up. The greater the passion, the more fortitude you can muster in the face of problems.

Learn to tolerate pain. Nothing worthwhile comes easy. Success always lies upstream, and you have to swim against the flow to reach it. If you wish to be persistent, you must be willing to tolerate discomfort patiently. Working past the pain helps you remain committed for the long haul. Remember the famous adage: 'no pain, no gain'.

Athletes have a unique relationship with pain. While human nature is to run away from discomfort and seek pleasure, world-class athletes do the reverse. Pushing themselves beyond extreme soreness is the price they pay for extraordinary accomplishments. Their inner fortitude is even more admirable than their external muscles. Mahatma Gandhi had said: 'Strength does not come from physical capacity. It comes from an indomitable will.'

Develop a never-say-die spirit and confidently face tough situations to come out victorious!

HOW TO STOP PROCRASTINATION

Question: Swamiji, I tend to delay acting on important things, much to my detriment later. How can I overcome this habit of procrastination?

Answer: 'Procrastination' means putting off important tasks until the last minute or even beyond the deadline. The reasons for postponing are usually trivial things and easily available pleasures that serve as distractions. Deferment, unfortunately, negatively impacts our projects, assignments, and chores. In the long run, postponement leads to remorse, as we fail to achieve important goals. Sidney Harris had said: 'Regret for the things we did can be tempered with time; it is the regret for things we did not do that is inconsolable.'

Little wonder that there are thousands of books to help people overcome procrastination. Let us quickly get to the root of it. Why do we still dawdle, even though we know it is a bad habit?

Our human brain values immediate rewards more than future ones. Suppose a student has an upcoming exam, and she knows studying hard will bestow enduring benefits. However, the pleasure of playing video games is immediate. Its lure, therefore, is more enticing than the long-term rewards of hard work. The intellect knows not studying could lead to bad grades or even flunking the exam. But these are in the distant future, while gratification from video games is immediate.

How long do we delay things? We tend to keep postponing until we perceive that the future pain from avoiding the task has become more than the gratification from the diversion. The same student, who was procrastinating earlier, now puts down her PlayStation the night before the exam. The possibility of experiencing pain from failing the exam immediately before her is more tangible than the pleasure from games.

The *Kaṭhopaniṣhad* describes the same concept of immediate versus delayed gratification. *Śhreya* happiness appears bitter in the short-term but finally turns into nectar. *Preya* pleasure is the opposite—it seems like ambrosia initially but proves to be poisonous later. The *Kaṭhopaniṣhad* (1.2.1–2) states:

> There are two paths—one is the 'beneficial' and the other is the 'pleasant'. These two lead to very different ends. The pleasant is enjoyable in the beginning but ends in pain. The ignorant are ensnared in it and perish. But the wise are not deceived by its attractions; they choose the beneficial and finally attain happiness.

Having understood your brain's proclivity, here are some ways to overcome the lure of procrastination. Use these to pursue important and enduring goals in life.

Reframe your thoughts. A lot of times, people dilly-dally because the task in front seems agonizing. You have a lengthy report to write that appears too boring. You have an important customer call to make, and you are anxious about how it will go. Your mind abjures the unpleasantness of the thing to do, and then you postpone it.

Avoid the mental trap by reframing your attitude towards the disagreeable work. Look for the enjoyable side of it. Often, when we get to the task, we realize it was not so unbearable after all.

Focus on your 'why'. As was explained, we procrastinate because the mind is interested in short-term happiness, or *preya*. Counter it by repeatedly reminding yourself about the benefits of completing the task. 'If I save money now, I will be able to plan a family vacation next year. But if I am thriftless now, I will have to forgo the holiday trip.' Keep reminding yourself of the reason 'why' what you set out to do is so important.

Reward and punish yourself sooner. We delay because the reward for the action is very far into the future. Likewise, the punishment for not doing it comes much later. What if you rewarded and penalized yourself in the shorter term?

For example, suppose you have a college assignment to complete which will take several days of research and writing. Break it into smaller chunks. Then reward yourself every time you complete a chunk. Tell yourself, 'I will only watch my favourite show if I complete this bit of my project today.' By doing so, the prize will come sooner. Consequently, your intellect will work for the immediate reward long before the entire assignment is complete.

Though these are effective techniques for overcoming procrastination, to implement them you will need another special virtue of character. What is that? Self-discipline. This is the personality trait that bridges the gap between intention and accomplishment. **With self-control, you can stop your mind from indulging in immediate pleasures. Without willpower, you will fall prey to every alluring distraction that comes your way.**

This naturally leads to the next question. What is the way for cultivating self-discipline?

HOW TO DEVELOP WILLPOWER

Question: I am painfully aware of my weaknesses and wish to correct them. But I have no willpower and keep repeating the same bad choices again and again. How can I strengthen my willpower?

Answer: Self-improvement is hard work that requires commitment and self-abnegation. These traits do not come easily. You will need to exert your willpower—not once, but again and again. You will have to forsake easily available pleasures and embrace austerities. Then, the fine goal of character development will become tangible.

Willpower is the attribute of your personality that empowers you to do the right thing, even though it is inconvenient. It helps you keep your tongue in check, your senses under control, and your mind focussed. When you unleash the force of your willpower, you become literally unstoppable in life. It is a key virtue to possess.

So, make it a priority to develop an abundance of self-restraint. It will help you eradicate many weaknesses from your personality. Let us now see how this can be done.

'Use it or lose it'. This is a simple principle of Nature—if you stop using a body part, it starts withering.

The phenomenon of atrophy is well known to anyone who has had a wrist fracture that required a plaster cast. The relevant joint remained in the cast—immobile for four weeks—and finally, when the cast was removed, one discovered that the wrist was frozen.

Disuse of the joint led to its atrophy. Months of physiotherapy and exercise were then required to regain regular motion of the joint.

The nature of the human body is 'use it or lose it'. Any part that stops getting used begins to regress. The practice of yogasanas is a very effective antidote for physical atrophy. Yogic postures flex our joints, tissues, and muscles, thereby toning them. Realizing this, the Western world has wholeheartedly embraced yoga for health and well-being.

The principle of atrophy applies to the brain as well. After retirement, people who lead inactive lives become susceptible to dementia. Their cerebrum gradually withers with disuse. Professors, in contrast, retain their intellectual and cognitive abilities well into their nineties because they keep using these faculties.

Willpower behaves in a similar fashion. It gets emaciated with disuse. Every time you give in to your lower nature against the wisdom of your intellect, you weaken your self-control by a strand. Fortunately for us, the reverse is also true. What is that?

Exercise the willpower muscle to make it stronger. You can grow your self-discipline just as you would build your biceps. When you exert your muscles beyond a point, they break and develop micro tears. But do not worry. In 48 hours, if you have taken the necessary nutrition, they mend and grow stronger than before.

Likewise, to develop your willpower muscle, exercise it with repeated acts of self-control. Developing self-discipline, therefore, is like constructing a house—it is built one brick at a time.

Initially, the strong gravitational pull of old habits will resist change. The phenomenon is quite similar to putting a rocket into space. The first few seconds of the launch consume the most fuel, as the rocket breaks through the earth's gravity. Expect the same when you consciously begin the flight to willpower mastery.

Start by making small resolutions and sticking to them—like refusing to scratch and relieve an itch or excluding all sweets from your diet. Every little victory will add up in breaking the grip of your baser instincts and freeing your higher nature. The trick is to keep raising the bar and gaining momentum. Soon, you will be flying high on the wings of self-control.

The good news is that willpower gained in any one sphere of your life becomes available in other spheres as well. So, do not delay. Set up your personal willpower challenge today and resolve to live a disciplined lifestyle.

One of the best exercises for the self-control muscle is meditation. It entails restraining the mind from pleasure-seeking thoughts and weaning it back to aspired ones. Hence, meditation is a powerful workout for your willpower muscle. Neurological research has revealed that a mere one hour of meditation, when practised for a month, can radically change the configuration of your brain. I have elaborated on this topic in great detail in my book, *7 Mindsets for Success, Happiness and Fulfilment.* You can refer to it for a deeper understanding of willpower.

3

Professional Mastery Skills

ACHIEVING FOCUS AT WORK

Question: I am not as productive as I would like to be because I often find myself losing focus at work. I easily get distracted by social media and other things that are more fun. But I see my colleagues working happily, completely immersed in their work. How can I also achieve that kind of absorption?

Answer: The ability to focus deeply on a task is a key skill not only for professional competence but also in performing mundane everyday tasks. However, with the constant deluge of distractions in the form of text messages, social media, and emails, this has become harder to achieve.

Why do we love distractions? They provide a 'dopamine kick' to the brain that results in instant gratification. That is why we turn to them, when 1) the task at hand is boring, or 2) it is so overwhelming that we find it difficult to even begin. Either way, we lose focus on work. Productivity suffers, and we feel discouraged.

Conversely, we also experience days of deep absorption when we are completely immersed in our work, without even noticing the clock. The hours go by, and we produce great work effortlessly. Think of the thousands of lines of software code you wrote with perfect focus, losing all track of time. Or perhaps the difficult project that took days to complete. Yet, you enjoyed every bit of it because you were so lost in the process.

What I have just described is the state of 'flow'. It is characterized by complete absorption in one's work. This results in an accompanying feeling of euphoria and unusual creativity. The story of Leo Tolstoy, the famous Russian writer, enchantingly illustrates this state.

Tolstoy was working on the plot of a novel. Deeply absorbed in it, he would even visualize the characters around him. Once, he was walking up an open flight of stairs, while someone else was descending from above. Tolstoy stepped to the side and fell off.

The other person asked, 'Why did you step aside? There was enough space for the two of us!'

Tolstoy replied, 'I was imagining the heroine of my book walking next to me. Mentally, I made space to accommodate both you and her, and I walked over to the side.'

Tolstoy's absorption in his work was so intense that he had lost all sense of his surroundings. Such a level of focus not only multiplies productivity but also makes work a very enjoyable experience. Hungarian–American psychologist, Mihaly Csikszentmihalyi, coined the term 'flow' to describe it. He also did tremendous research identifying the factors that help achieve it. Let us see what they are.

Match your skills with the task at hand. If the work is too easy, you will not be challenged and could feel bored. Conversely, if the work is too hard, it could stress you out. But when the difficulty level matches your skillset, your intellect will be fully engaged. Then, the propensity for distractions will reduce.

Work on one task at a time. Pick a specific task that you are going to work on—be it writing a blog, planning a presentation, designing a logo, or whatever else you choose to do—and stick to it. Otherwise, you will be inclined to switch between tasks and will easily get distracted with nothing to show.

Have a clear outcome in mind. Be clear about what you want to accomplish and the steps involved. This will enable you to continually evaluate how you are doing. Often, it is enough to prevent the mind from wandering or quitting.

Avoid distractions in the environment. These are the primary enemies of flow. At least 10 to 15 minutes of undivided time is necessary before you can get into a flow. Diversions will subvert the process. So, turn off your phone and television, and work in a quiet place.

Achieving flow is the perfect way to enjoy your work and also be your most productive self. It is a state that keeps you focussed on the present moment, empowering you to produce your best.

PRACTICE VS DELIBERATE PRACTICE

Question: I have considerable work experience. I have been practising my craft for many years. Now, I want to become an elite performer. What is the best way to do this?

Answer: Proficiency in any field requires consistent and steady practice. The world's greatest surgeons, musicians, athletes, and professionals, all achieved mastery through innumerable hours of training. 'Practice makes perfect' is an aphorism that we all know, and hence, this is not a new suggestion. However, there is a caveat here. **The quantity of practice does not suffice; quality of training makes the difference. This is called 'deliberate practice'.**

Why is quality important? Understand through an example.

Let us assume you start playing the game of golf. Initially, you learn the basic strokes and how to avoid simple mistakes. Shortly after 50 hours of practice, you can hit the ball with some success. Now, you think less about each shot and play from habit. Then learning tapers off.

This is because on reaching a certain level of competence, the skill becomes automatic. You can then play your shots mindlessly. At this point, additional time on the golf course only helps maintain your skills, not improve them.

Why has progress tapered off? Because from any one given location, you play only a single shot. You do not get a chance to evaluate your mistakes or correct them. Instead, if you played multiple shots from the same location, it would give you the opportunity to assess and adjust your technique, thereby improving your game.

This is how professionals train—they repeatedly practise the same shot again and again, while noticing their mistakes and correcting them. The same principle applies to the mastery of all skills. Long years of experience in a craft do not guarantee superior performance. On the contrary, familiarity and experience can even make one complacent. Doctors who have practised for 20 years are sometimes less proficient than those with seven years of experience because they feel they have reached an acceptable level of competence. They believe their skills are 'good enough' and do not strive to improve them further.

Mastery is achieved through deliberate practice. This is training with an energetic effort to improve. In it, you work on your weaknesses and extend the range of your skills. Then, there is constant progress and expertise develops.

Achieving elite performance requires continuous self-evaluation and the struggle to improve. It is a painful process from which most people shy away. As a result, only a small percentage of people reach the expert level in any field.

Here are the steps involved in deliberate practice.

Identify an area of weakness. The first step is to pinpoint your deficiency or lack of current ability. Now, set a goal to improve it. For example, you could decide that public speaking is your weakness, and you want to develop this skill.

Break down your goal into smaller, tangible tasks. The principle behind deliberate practice is to achieve small and realistic steps for improvement. For example, to improve your public speaking skills, you may want to work on eye coordination, hand gestures, voice projection, opening hook, and so forth.

Give each task your full attention. Every specific activity you identified now needs focussed attention. Set aside dedicated and uninterrupted time to work on each item. Make it your focussed goal to train with the intention to improve.

You may find that you tire out after just two hours of concentrated practice. This is natural; your intellect is engaged in performing and refining simultaneously. Your brain is stretching itself beyond its limits. Be reassured, however, that two hours of purposeful training is more fruitful than a week of mindless repetition.

Get out of your comfort zone. Deliberate practice is not always enjoyable. You are forcing yourself to do something that is difficult because it is beyond your current capacity. But you have identified it as essential for mastery, so start with baby steps.

For example, if you are practising a presentation, first do so in front of a mirror, then in front of your family. After this, request a peer to watch your presentation. Later, move to a small group of trusted individuals before the actual presentation. Doing so will gradually develop your confidence and finesse.

Seek feedback. One critical component of deliberate practice is receiving feedback from a coach, peer, or mentor. Their constructive advice will help you identify areas of improvement. Consider asking them: 'Am I conveying the message clearly?', 'Is the content gripping and interesting?', 'How can I make it more energetic and appealing?', and so on. Request them to point out mistakes and shortcomings of your speech. Now, you can integrate the learning to perfect your presentation.

You can apply these principles of deliberate practice to achieve expert performance in any field. This is what will set you apart from the crowd.

BALANCING PROFESSIONAL AND MATERIAL LIFE

Question: How do we balance our time-intensive academic and professional obligations with spiritual pursuits?

Answer: Let us take inspiration from elevated saints in history. Did you know that many of them were also great kings, generals, musicians, and writers? Parikshit, Prahalad, Ambarish, Prithu, and Janak were some of the greatest Saints mentioned in the scriptures. Yet, they were also exemplary kings—perfect in their profession, which entailed administration of a large kingdom.

Dhruv Maharaj was a devotee of God from childhood and went on to rule a vast nation. As a monarch, he flawlessly fulfilled his obligations towards his citizens, and yet, was also perfectly spiritual.

Yudhishthir, another great devotee and king, fought one of the most terrifying wars in history. Imagine how much more complex his situation would have been. If Yudhishthir could engage in bhakti on a battlefield, then surely we can incorporate it into our life as well.

No wonder Shree Krishna chose the setting of a battle to impart the timeless wisdom of the Bhagavad Gita. He conveyed the strong message that spirituality can be practised along with time-intensive occupations. The technique Shree Krishna taught is called 'Karm Yog'. Let us see what it is.

Presently, while working, our mind does not remain equipoised. We harbour anger, fear, stress, tension, anxiety, and innumerable other thoughts and sentiments. This is the antithesis of the state of yog. The Bhagavad Gita guides one to be in yog even while working. 'Yog' means 'union of the consciousness'. When our consciousness is filled with loving devotional thoughts of God, it is called yog. And if we can retain such consciousness even while working, it becomes karm yog.

Karm yog is basically *karm* (action) plus *yog* (mind attached to God), meaning, 'Do your worldly works with your body while keeping the mind in God at all times.' The second part of this instruction is difficult—to always keep the mind on the Divine. Many of us do remember God when we do pooja in the morning, but after the pooja is over, we forget Him for the rest of the day. We must now try to remember the Lord at all times. How?

Practise feeling the presence of God. Throughout our waking state, we constantly perceive ourselves, 'I am eating, I am walking, I am thinking, I am speaking, etc.' We are conscious of 'I am' but forget to realize 'God is also with me'.

We must now add this perception to our consciousness: 'I am not alone. My Soul-Beloved is always accompanying me. He is my Witness and Protector.' In fact, God is everywhere and all-pervading, but we have forgotten to realize His presence. Now we need to make space for Him in our awareness and practise realizing His constant presence with us.

How to perceive God's presence while working. Let us say, you go to your office and sit on your chair in the morning. Take a pause before you start work. First, make God sit on an empty chair in one corner of the room. Think, 'Shree Krishna is watching me. All I am doing is for His pleasure and in His service.' Now, begin your work.

Since we are not yet accomplished, it is natural that as we get engrossed in our work, God will slip out of our mind. Never mind. After an hour, stop work, and think, 'God is watching me. He is saying, "Aay...you were supposed to keep your mind in Me. What have you started thinking?"' In this way, our consciousness that had slipped will again be uplifted. The stream of poor thoughts that had begun flowing in our mind will stop.

We must keep practising in this manner after every hour. Once we have established the practice at intervals of one hour, then increase the frequency to every half hour. When that is achieved, increase the frequency further to intervals of 15 minutes. With constant practice, we will reach a stage where we continuously feel the presence of God with us.

sarveṣhu kāleṣhu mām anusmara yudhya cha

(Bhagavad Gita verse 8.7)

Shree Krishna tells Arjun to continue fighting the righteous war because, as a warrior, it is his duty. But along with it, he should also strive to remember God at all times. Simply put, karm yog can be described as 'mind in God, body at work'.

The technique of karm yog bestows many benefits.

First, we see ourselves as fragments of the Divine. Such an attitude allows us to develop a healthy self-identity, not based on ego or who people think we are, but on the reality of our soul. We maintain humility without being self-demeaning.

Second, we see our work as service to the Divine. The work becomes not drudgery to go through, but a joy to perform. Since our work is for the pleasure of God, we exert ourselves with a positive attitude and to the best of our ability.

Third, since the results of our efforts are for the pleasure of the Supreme, we are not attached to them. If we do not get the desired results despite our best exertions, we think, 'Probably, it was not the will of the Lord. Let me submit to His wish and be happy.' This sense of detachment frees us from stress, anxiety, tension, and fear.

Fourth, we view everyone with whom we interact as divine fragments of God and consequently maintain a healthy attitude towards them. Our interpersonal interactions are positive and service-oriented.

Fifth, when we keep God in our consciousness, we realize that His grace makes all things possible, and, in turn, we become free from the pride of doership.

Sixth, the goal of human life is God-realization. In karm yog, we move towards this goal together with doing our worldly duties.

However, to achieve mastery in karm yog, you will also need to give up karm for an hour every day, so you can engage in intensive sadhana in isolation. This is explained in the question 'The Need for Daily Sadhana'.

Thus, we see that setting a fixed time aside for daily sadhana is essential. It helps to focus and purify the mind and uplift our consciousness for the day.

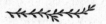

4

Mind Management Skills

MIND SWINGS BETWEEN GUNAS

Question: I have trouble implementing your teachings as my mind constantly keeps fluctuating between sattva, rajas, and tamas. It's hard to keep it in a meditative state. Please guide me.

Answer: For the mind to oscillate between the three gunas is but natural. Let us understand the reason why. These gunas—sattva, rajas, and tamas—are present in the material energy, maya. Our mind is also made from maya. Hence, all three gunas are present in our mind as well. They can be compared to three wrestlers competing with each other. Each keeps throwing the other down. Sometimes one is on top and sometimes the other.

A similar tussle among the three gunas takes place in our mind. One or the other guna begins to dominate, depending upon the environment and our own chintan (contemplation). For example, if you visit a temple, the sacred environs make your mind sattvic. Subsequently, you spend time playing tennis with your friends. Rajas and the spirit of competition now dominate your thoughts. Then you go and attend a friend's party. The conversation and late-night hour enhance tamas in your mind.

Notice how your mind has been swinging amongst the gunas with the changing circumstances. Whichever guna rules your mind, the corresponding thoughts and emotions dominate your consciousness.

These changing modes influence one's devotional sentiments as well.

- When the mode of goodness becomes prominent, we start thinking, 'God and Guru are so benevolent. They have blessed me in so many ways. I must show gratitude by sincerely engaging in bhakti.'
- When the mode of passion rules, we think, 'What is the hurry to do bhakti? I have many responsibilities now, and they are more important.'
- When the mode of ignorance dominates, we think, 'I am not sure if there is any God or not, for no one has ever seen Him. So why waste time in bhakti?'

Notice how our thoughts oscillate from such heights to such depths in a fraction of a moment. But do not let this constant fluctuation of the gunas deject you. Instead, accept that this is natural, and then work to rise above it.

Sadhana means to fight the flow of the three gunas and to force the mind to maintain the highest devotional emotions. The *Bhakti Śhatak* states:

mana māyā te hī banyo, māyā te saṅsār
yāte mana bhāvat sadā, yah saṅsār asār (verse 36)

'The mind is made from maya, and so is the world. Hence, for the mind to be inclined towards the world is only expected.'

Sadhana means to counter the mind's natural disposition with our intellect. We must force the mind against its lower nature to harbour divine emotions. This is a two-step process:

- First, remove the mind from the world.
- Second, force the mind to focus upon God.

Both these steps will require effort, but do not be discouraged. With practice, it will grow easier. This is just as driving a car is difficult initially, but with training, it becomes natural.

The goal of sadhana is to rise to the transcendental state beyond the three gunas. These gunas are active agents of maya. But the Supreme Lord is beyond them. He is, therefore, called *triguṇātīt* (beyond the gunas). Similarly, His Names, Forms, Virtues, Pastimes, Abodes, and Associates are also *triguṇātīt*.

When, through sadhana, the mind gets attached to God, it transcends the gunas and becomes divine as well. Then the tussle of the three gunas gets completely vanquished from our mind.

HOW TO SUSTAIN MOTIVATION

Question: How do we keep our motivation on the spiritual path if we do not see any progress? And what are the signs of progress in any case?

Answer: Everything worthwhile and noble requires sustained effort. A bamboo tree takes approximately five years to grow. Likewise, the spiritual journey is a lengthy one. We must not be discouraged if the desired results do not come right away but should continue to strive enthusiastically if we aspire to reach the goal.

Enthusiasm is the antidote to discouragement; it is the fuel that propels us forward. Maharishi Patanjali emphasized it in sutra 1.21 in his *Yog Darshan*: *tīvra saṁvegānāmāsannaḥ* 'Endeavour for spiritual elevation with great energy.'

So, **how do we generate and sustain great enthusiasm within ourselves?** Inspiration for any activity comes from the importance our intellect accords to it. For example, if you decide a project presentation you need to make to your company board is critical to your career, you will be inspired to put in your best efforts. This is because your intellect believes it is extremely important for you.

But if your intellect believes, 'It really does not matter how the presentation goes', your motivation to do your best will also wane. Likewise, callousness in sadhana comes when we forget the opportunity the current moment presents. We begin thinking, 'What is the hurry? I still have another 50 years to live.'

Speed develops when we remind ourselves that we have received the human form after many births in the 8.4 million species of life. It is a golden chance to reach the supreme destination of the soul. In addition, we must also remember that human life is transient. It can be snatched away at any moment by death. Hence, we must not delay in our efforts at sadhana. Narayan

Swami states:

do bātan ko bhūl mat, jo chāhasi kalyāṇ
nārāyaṇ ek maut ko, dūjo śhrī bhagavān

He says, 'To succeed in sadhana, do not forget two things. First, remember your death, and then, remember God.' The idea of remembering death is to create a sense of urgency.

In conclusion, we will stay enthusiastic if we keep these two principles in our awareness: 1) human life is precious and 2) human life is temporary.

Now, coming to the second part of your question, what are the signs for evaluating spiritual advancement?

The first indicator of progress is increasing detachment from the world. When you are detached, you possess the ability to maintain mental poise amid hardships. You are able to manage your emotions so much so that you maintain your composure even when there is a reason to be angry. You are better able to tolerate insults and hurts. As your desires subside, you experience greater inner peace and equanimity.

Besides, detachment from results will make you stress-free, even while putting in your best efforts. Consequently, you will become a positive thinker, neither elated by material pleasures nor dejected by pain.

The second sign of progress is a growing attachment to God. This will manifest in a longing for satsang. You will experience unbounded enthusiasm for spiritual practices and activities. These will be accompanied by sweet transcendental bliss from within; a consequence of the mind connecting with the Ocean of bliss, which is God.

You can consider these as symptoms that your mind is coming under control. Your consciousness is becoming less worldly and more spiritual. These positive transformations will further increase your faith in the process. Then, with enhanced faith, when you strive, you will progress even more rapidly. That will give you more results, which will grow your faith even further. And you will do sadhana with even more enthusiasm. In this way, you will one day reach your supreme goal.

PEACE IN ADVERSE CIRCUMSTANCES

Question: I feel deeply disturbed and dejected in adverse situations. How can I insulate my mind from circumstances and remain at peace?

Answer: The world we live in is full of dualities. There is summer and winter, day and night, success and failure. In the journey of life, we inevitably encounter changing circumstances. How do we respond? When things are favourable, we become happy. However, when circumstances turn antagonistic, we get disturbed. Negative thoughts fill the mind, and we lose our peace.

When this happens, we blame the externals for our unhappy thoughts. 'My boss reprimanded me', 'The neighbour irritates me', 'The economy is not doing well', and so on. We feel situations are the reason for our bad mood.

Instead, **realize the gap between your mind and the externals.** No matter what the circumstance, you are free to choose your emotional response. The outside world is not in your control, but your inner world is. Take inspiration from this incident told by Sundar Pichai, CEO of Google.

Sundar Pichai related this experience while he was at a restaurant for dinner. On the next table was an amiable group of aged people. Suddenly, a cockroach flew in and sat on the neck of a lady in the group. She panicked and stood up, screaming at peak decibels, hoping the insect would fly away.

Her shrieks scared the poor vermin. It took flight and this time landed on an aged gentleman's forehead. It was now his turn to get up and yell. This began a chain reaction. Each time the cockroach would find a new landing ground, it turned out to be equally noisy.

While this drama was unfolding, a waiter walked in to check what the commotion was about. The cockroach, in the meantime, flew again and landed on the waiter's tie. The waiter responded differently from the elderly group. He retained his composure and allowed the insect to settle down. Then, he grabbed it with a napkin and threw it out of the restaurant.

Observing this pandemonium got Pichai thinking. What was the cause of everyone's agitation? Could it have been the cockroach? If so, why was the waiter not disturbed? And if the waiter could remain equanimous, why did the others get so agitated? Pichai then concluded that it was not the situation but the inability to handle it, which led to their overblown reaction.

Likewise, if we get agitated by our manager's shouting or a traffic jam, the situations are not to blame. It is our reaction to situations that creates chaos in our mind. The problem gets compounded because we do not realize it is within us. We point fingers at others for our moods and blame circumstances for our unhappiness. Now, we need the external situation to change to get into a good mood. This effectively takes away the key to our emotions from us.

However, this is an immature way of thinking. If children blame others for their moods, it is understandable. But as grown-ups, we are expected to be emotionally responsible. To achieve this, we have to decouple our mind from the environment, realize our God-given freedom to choose our thoughts, and then use that freedom to choose happy and optimistic emotions.

Learn from the examples of successful people in history who also had their share of disappointments and failures, and yet, remained positive in their attitude and productive in their profession. For example,

- Soordas was blind from birth.
- Saint Kabir was of unknown parentage.
- Saint Ravidas was thrown out of his home in adolescence.
- Tulsidas had people trying to kill him.

Likewise in the material realm:

- Beethoven was almost deaf when he created his best compositions.
- Stephen Hawking was physically challenged most of his life.
- Hellen Keller lost her hearing and sight when she was just 18 months old.

These great personalities displayed the ability to take charge of their attitudes and make the best of what they had received.

The key takeaway here is that undesirable things do happen. Life does not always serve us chocolates and cakes; it also sends lemons our way. But do lemons turn us sour or do we make lemonade out of them? This depends on our ability to manage our emotions.

As the saying goes: 'Two men looked out from the prison bars. One saw mud, the other saw stars.'

If the great saints and brilliant luminaries who blazed the earth had brooded over the list of items that God had not bestowed upon them, they would have died in bitterness. Instead, they took charge of their attitudes and made the best of what they did receive. So, let us learn to do the same and accept all circumstances and events as a blessing from Above.

5

Philosophy

GOD IS THE DOER VS WE ARE RESPONSIBLE

Question: The scriptures tell us that we are the doers of our actions. On the other hand, they also tell us that God is the doer. Which statement is correct? Are 'we' the doer or is 'God' the doer?

Answer: The scriptures do appear to make contradictory statements on this point. In some places, they say that we are responsible for our deeds.

nādatte kasyachit pāpaṁ na chaiva sukṛitaṁ vibhuḥ

(Bhagavad Gita 5.15)

'The omnipresent God does not involve Himself in the sinful or virtuous deeds of anyone.'

In other places, the same scripture states that God is the doer.

sarvasya chāhaṁ hṛidi sanniviṣhṭo
mattaḥ smṛitir jñānam apohanaṁ cha

(Bhagavad Gita 15.15)

'I am seated in the hearts of all living beings, and from Me come memory, knowledge, as well as forgetfulness.'

These are apparently contradictory viewpoints, but actually, this is not the case. Let us understand how.

God bestows us with the energy to perform actions. Alongside, He also gives us the freedom to use that energy in any way we wish. This is the free will to make choices.

For example, the electrical station supplies electricity to our home. If it did not give power, we would not be able to use electrical appliances. Now, once we have that power, we have the choice of using it as we wish—we could heat our home, cool it, even touch the wrong wires and electrocute ourselves. Whatever we do, we cannot blame the electrical station for it because the use of electricity was in our hands.

Similarly, God energizes our eyes with vision. If He did not give us this power, we would not be able to see anything. But how we use the gift of sight is a decision we make for ourselves. We could use our eyes to see the divine form of God in a temple, or we could sit in a theatre and watch a movie.

Thus, **we utilize our free will to make choices.** We cannot blame God and say, 'Why does He make me watch these movies?' That would be unjustified. God simply bestows the power of sight. How we utilize our eyes is left to our discretion. The same applies to the other senses and the mind as well.

In this way, there are two kinds of doers:

- *Prayojak kartā* is the one who bestows the power to perform actions. This is God.
- *Prayojya kartā* is the one who uses the power, as he/she

deems fit. This is the individual soul.

Hence, both the statements of the scriptures are correct regarding the doer of activities. God is the doer because He is the *prayojak kartā*. The soul is also the doer because it is the *prayojya kartā*.

In determining responsibility for actions, *prayojya kartā* is the primary factor—the one who exercises free will. The soul, therefore, is held responsible for its karmas. Thus, as per the Law of Karma, it reaps the results.

Only the works of sharanagat (surrendered souls) saints can be attributed to God. This is because they have aligned their will with God's will. As a result, the Supreme is now the doer of their actions. He makes them a conduit for His divine work in the world. Such souls can say:

na maiṅ kiyā na kari sakauñ, sahib karatā mor
karat karāvat āp hai, tulasi tulasi śhor

Saint Tulsidas says: 'People are crediting me for writing the *Ramcharitmanas*. However, I have neither composed it nor do I have the ability to do so. Bhagavan Ram inspired me and got it done. The world is unaware of this fact, and hence, they are acclaiming "Tulsidas! Tulsidas!"'

So, remember, that until we reach the point where we are fully surrendered to God, we will remain the doers. We will be held responsible for the choices we make and the actions we perform.

REINCARNATION

Question: My friends in school completely reject the concept of reincarnation. Is rebirth a fact or just a myth?

Answer: The soul is eternal—it existed even before birth and will continue to exist even after death. There is, in fact, no birth or death for the soul. 'Death' is merely the act of discarding its old dysfunctional body. And what is called 'birth' is the soul receiving a new body to continue its journey. This principle of the soul changing bodies is called 'reincarnation'.

The Bhagavad Gita explains reincarnation beautifully. It states that in this life itself, we continually change bodies:

dehino 'smin yathā dehe kaumāraṁ yauvanaṁ jarā
tathā dehāntara-prāptir dhīras tatra na muhyati (2.13)

'Just as the embodied soul continuously passes from childhood to youth to old age, similarly, at the time of death, the soul passes into another body. The wise are not deluded by this.'

What wonderful logic! Reincarnation is happening in this life itself—the body is continuously changing.

The *Nyāya Darshan* also gives strong evidence for rebirth. It states that a one-month-old baby, without any visible reason, experiences the emotions of happiness, sadness, and fear:

jātasya harṣhabhayaśhoka sampratipatteḥ (3.1.18)

Sometimes, the little infant smiles without a cause. At other times, it cries or becomes fearful, again without reason. These emotions arise because of past life memories that are still not fully erased.

Without accepting reincarnation, it is impossible to explain the disparity that exists among human beings. For example, how can one explain why someone is born blind? If we say it was the will of God, the question arises: Why did the all-merciful God do injustice to a particular soul? If we say it was the result of karmas, the question will arise regarding when these karmas were performed by a newborn. Since this baby was just born, it obviously means that its actions cannot be of this lifetime; it is evident the actions had to be of prior lives. The principle of reincarnation offers the only reasonable answer to the disparity of births. In verse 2.22 of the Bhagavad Gita, Shree Krishna states:

vāsānsi jīrṇāni yathā vihāya navāni grihṇāti naro 'parāṇi
tathā śharīrāṇi vihāya jīrṇānya nyāni sanyāti navāni dehī

'As a person sheds worn-out garments and wears new ones, likewise, at the time of death, the soul casts off its worn-out body and enters a new one.'

The concept of reincarnation is not unique to Vedic scriptures. It is accepted in most Eastern philosophies. It is an inherent part of Hinduism, Jainism, and Sikhism. In Buddhism, we see that Lord Buddha made frequent references to his past lives.

In ancient classical Western religious and philosophic circles, famous thinkers, such as Pythagoras, Plato, and Socrates accepted reincarnation to be true, and their views were also reflected in Orphism, Hermeticism, Neoplatonism, Manichaenism, and Gnosticism.

Within the mainstream Abrahamic faiths as well, many mystics of the three major religions supported reincarnation. Josephus, the great ancient Jewish historian, used language in his writings that ascribes belief in some form of reincarnation among the Pharisees and Essenes of his day. The Jewish Kabbalah prescribes to the idea of reincarnation as *gilgul neshamot*, or the 'rolling of the soul'.

Many of the early Christians believed in the concept of reincarnation. Jesus indirectly proclaimed this doctrine when he told his disciples that John the Baptist was Elijah the Prophet reincarnated (Matthew 11:13–14). Solomon's 'Book of Wisdom' says: 'To be born in a sound body with sound limbs is a reward of the virtues of past lives.'[1]

The great Sufi mystic Jalal al-Din Muhammad Rumi declared[2]:

> I died as stone, and rose again as plant;
> I died as plant and became an animal;
> I died as animal and was born a man
> ...
> Yet once more shall I die as man,
> to soar with angels blessed above.

Thus, most of the major religions have direct or indirect references to the concept of reincarnation.

---

[1]Dass, Ram, *Paths to God: Living the Bhagavad Gita*, Harmony, New York, 2007, Kindle ebook.
[2]Ibid.

REMEMBERING OUR PAST LIVES

Question: Why don't we remember our past lives, Swamiji? There have been times, probably in my childhood, when I got the feeling of déjà vu. It felt like I had seen something or some place before, as if possibly from a previous life.

Answer: In the previous question, we discussed that the present life is not our first one. We have taken birth innumerable times before this one as well. Now, let us see what happens at the time of death.

Every soul in the material realm is bound by three bodies—gross body, subtle body, and causal body. The technical names for them are *sthūl śharīr*, *sūkṣhma śharīr,* and *kāraṇ śharīr.* At the time of death, the soul discards its gross body and departs with the subtle and causal bodies.

However, the process of death is very painful for the soul. It wipes away memories of the life gone by. Subsequently, the process of birth is even more painful. These two episodes erase literally all recollections of the past. Hence, the common norm is that people do not remember their previous lives. Yet, there have been exceptions in all cultures of the world—people who remembered an earlier lifetime.

The famous true story of Shanti Devi supports the theory of reincarnation. Shanti Devi (1926–87) was born in Delhi. Her official biography has been documented in a book titled, I Have Lived Before, written by a Swedish journalist, Sture Lonnerstrand. Dozens of other books have also been published about her.

When Shanti Devi was about four years old, she told her family,

'This is not my real home! I have a son and a husband in Mathura! I must go back to them!' Her family initially paid very little attention to her words, but Shanti persisted.

Her teacher proceeded to inquire into the matter. He discovered that there was actually a Kedar Nath Pandey in Mathura as Shanti Devi had claimed. His wife, Lugdi Devi, had passed away 10 days after giving birth to a son. This incident had happened 14 months before Shanti Devi was born.

Kedar Nath then travelled to Delhi, pretending to be his own brother. Shanti Devi, however, recognized him and reminded him of details from her past life. Mahatma Gandhi came to know of this and set up a 15-member commission of eminent people to probe Shanti's claims.

Along with the commission, Shanti travelled to Mathura. From the railway station, she sat on a horse cart, guiding the charioteer all the way to her old home. She even pointed out the new buildings that had come up. She recognized many of her old family members. But Shanti was disappointed that Kedar Nath had failed to keep many promises he had given on Lugdi Devi's deathbed.

The commission concluded that Shanti Devi was definitely a reincarnation of Lugdi Devi. She remained single all her life and never went to Mathura again.

People like Shanti Devi are exceptions. The common rule is that one forgets one's past life. As explained earlier, death and birth are so painful that they erase past life impressions.

Yet, some residual impressions remain in everyone's subconscious. These memories create a feeling of déjà vu. This is a French term for describing the strange feeling about something presently happening to you, which makes you sense you have seen it before.

Déjà vu occurs more in childhood. However, as we grow up, imprints of the present life get impressed very strongly on the mind. Then the feeling of déjà vu largely dies away.

DESTINY

Question: Are we controlled by our destiny, or can we change it by our actions?

Answer: To think that we are bound by destiny, which cannot be changed, is the doctrine of fatalism. This is how 'fatalism' is defined:

1. **Doctrine of fate:** The philosophical doctrine according to which all events are fated to happen, and human beings cannot change their destiny.
2. **Belief in all-powerful fate:** The belief that people are powerless against fate.
3. **Feeling of powerlessness against fate:** An attitude of resignation and passivity that results from the belief that people are helpless against fate.

We will analyse whether the tenets of fatalism are correct or not. First of all, let us understand what destiny is. The *Hitopadeśh* explains:

pūrva janma kṛitaṁ karma taddaivamiti kathyate

'The actions we performed in our past lives become our destiny in the present one.'

Bear this definition of destiny in mind. Fate, or destiny, is not simply a horoscope chart that is revealed to us by astrologers. We make it ourselves by our previous karmas. This means, in past lives, we performed actions by our free will.

Now, the question is whether we can change destiny or not. To derive the answer, I will use the technique of *reductio ad absurdum.*

- Let us start with the premise: *We are bound by destiny in this life.*
- The same premise would apply to past lives as well because all lives should be governed by the same set of rules.
- This implies: *In our past lives too, we were bound by destiny.*
- If the above holds true, then it means that we never performed any actions by our free volition in any previous lifetime.
- In that case, where did our destiny originate from?
- If we performed actions with our free will in any past life, then we can do so in our present life as well.

Thus, the premise that everything is predestined leads to logical absurdity and is disproved.

There is, undeniably, an element of *prārabdh* (destiny) in our life. But it is a creation of our own past karmas. There are three kinds of karmas appended to our soul: 1) *sañchit* karmas, 2) *prārabdh* karmas, and 3) *kriyamāṇ* karmas.

Sañchit karmas is the inventory of our karmas of endless lifetimes. God keeps an account of it. At the time of birth, when He sends us into the world, He gives us a portion of our *sañchit* karmas to enjoy or suffer. This portion is called *prārabdh* karma. The *prārabdh,* which is less than 10 per cent of karmas of present life, is fixed for the present life. But at every moment, we also have the freedom to perform works as we choose. These are called *kriyamāṇ* karmas—the actions we perform in the present by our free will.

The *prārabdh* is predetermined, but *kriyamāṇ* is not. It is in our hands and can be changed as we wish.

For example, it may be in someone's destiny to win a lottery worth one million dollars. But with hard work, they can either grow it ten-fold to 10 million dollars or become an alcoholic and blow it all away. We see, therefore, that destiny is fixed. But the present efforts are in our hands. And those present efforts are most important.

For instance, we saw how so many Indians made their mark in the recent 2020 Paralympics. Athletes with a range of disabilities participated. If you read about their life stories, many of them lost their limbs in some accident. It is quite possible the accident may have been in their destiny. But if they had just accepted it and not strived any further in life, they would not have been in the arena of international sports. Hence, it is said:

daiva daiva ālasī pukārā (Ramayan 5.50.2)

'It is lazy people who blame destiny for their substandard achievements.' Instead of focussing on performing their work properly, they keep running to astrologers to know their destiny. Then they superstitiously wear precious stones or worship Rahu and Shani for appeasement.

Instead of running to astrologers to know your destiny, focus on building it. The science of work is perfectly explained by this sutra:

prayatn mein sāvadhān aur phal mein santuṣhṭī

While putting in your efforts, do not bring destiny to your mind. Work as if the outcome depends upon you. But when you receive the results, accept it as fate. Remember that the results are not in your hands. In this way, you will work hard, and yet, not be disturbed by the outcome.

WHY WE CAME INTO THE WORLD

Question: If, at one time, we were with God in His divine Abode, then how did we become separate from Him and come to this world?

Answer: The question expresses a very common mistaken notion. It assumes we were once in *Golok*—God's divine Abode—and we fell down from there into this material world.

This, however, is incorrect and does not stand to reason. Had we been in the divine Abode once upon a time, we would have been relishing divine bliss. Why would we choose to reject perfect happiness for the puny material pleasures of this world? Also, in the divine realm, we would have been enlightened with divine knowledge. Then why would we choose to cover ourselves with the ignorance of maya?

We have not fallen into material existence from the divine Abode. The *maya baddh* (materially bound) soul has had its back towards God since eternity. This is called *vimukhtā*. In this state, under the grip of maya, we are continously rotating in the cycle of life and death.

We have been *vimukh* from God since eternity. However, He has granted us the freedom of choice. Our work is to use our free will to become *saṁmukh*—turn our face to God. This is the evolutionary journey of the soul, from *vimukhṭā* to *saṁmukhtā*, which God needs us to accomplish before He accepts us in His eternal divine Abode.

In the human form, we have a golden opportunity to complete that journey and reach the supreme perfection that the Lord has in store for us.

GOAL OF LIFE

Question: I am confused about the goal of life. Can you please help me understand it?

Answer: The human form you have received in this life is very special. It has been given to you for achieving a very important goal.

āhāra-nidrā-bhaya-maithunaṁ cha
sāmānyam etat paśhubhir narāṇām
jñānaṁ hi teṣhām adhiko viśheṣho
jñānena hīnāḥ paśhubhiḥ samānāḥ (*Hitopadeśh*)

Sage Bhartrihari states that even animals engage in eating, sleeping, mating, and defending. As humans, we have been specially blessed with the faculty of knowledge. We must use it for a higher purpose and not for animalistic activities alone. What is that higher goal?

A story is told about Swami Ram Tirth, who was amongst the first Indian spiritual teachers to travel to the West. He went to the US in 1902.

Swami Ram Tirth was travelling by sea to the US, and an Indian student was on the ship with him. The student was extremely proud that he was going abroad to study but had no appreciation of India's rich spiritual heritage. With utmost compassion, Swamiji decided to open his eyes. He asked the student, 'What are you going to America for?'

'To study engineering,' replied the student. 'I'll finish my BTech and return. Then I will get a high government job and get married to a beautiful girl. We will have children and raise them well. Alongside, I will engage in economic development. With the wealth I earn, I will have delicious food, sleep luxuriously, and live a secure life.'

Swami Ram Tirth heard his life plan and then explained, 'All the activities you have delineated fall into four categories—eating, sleeping, mating, and defending. But these are activities that even animals engage in. If your goal is simply to engage in deluxe animal life, there is no need for higher education.'

We eat 56 kinds of delicacies, while the cow grazes grass. But the activity of eating is the same. We rest on soft beds, while dogs rest on the earth. We mate and beget progeny, and animals do the same. We protect ourselves with savings and insurance policies, while animals defend themselves with fangs and claws.

Then, what distinguishes us from animals?

God has bestowed the faculty of knowledge—not merely eating, sleeping, mating, and defending—for a higher objective. We must use our God-given gift to know and attain the Absolute Truth. The *Kenopanishad* states:

iha chedavedīdatha satyamasti
na chedihāvedīnmahatī vinaṣhṭhiḥ (mantra 2.5)

'Oh Humans! In this human form, quickly strive to reach the Supreme Truth. Otherwise, you will suffer a great disaster.' What is that disaster? The human form will be snatched away upon death, and your soul will go back into the lower species of life.

That is why, **as human beings, we must strive to attain the ultimate evolutionary goal of the soul, which is God-realization.**

ATMA JNANA VS BRAHMA JNANA

Question: Swamiji, please explain what is atma jnana and brahma jnana. Also, what is the difference between self-realization and God-realization?

Answer: There are three entities in creation—Brahman, soul, and maya. Brahman is the all-powerful, all-knowing, and omnipresent God. He is the Creator, Maintainer, and Dissolver of the world. **Knowledge of God is called brahma jnana.**

Atma is the individual soul. It is a fragmental part of God. Like God, it is eternal; but unlike God, it is not all-powerful, all-knowing, or omnipresent. **Knowledge of the atma is called atma jnana.**

The Bhagavad Gita states:

mamaivānśho jīva-loke jīva-bhūtaḥ sanātanaḥ (verse 15.7)

Shree Krishna states: 'The embodied souls in this material world are My eternal fragmental parts.' Hence, **atma jnana is a tiny fraction of brahma jnana.**

Consider the analogy of the ocean and a drop of water. One who knows a single drop does not know the length and depth of the ocean. But one who has knowledge of the ocean automatically knows its drops as well.

In the same manner, the Vedas state:

ekasmin vijñāte sarvamidaṁ vijñātaṁ bhavati

'One who comes to know the Absolute Truth attains knowledge of everything.' **This means, if you become a brahma jnani, you will automatically become an atma jnani as well.** But the reverse cannot be said. If you possess atma jnana, it does not mean you also possess brahma jnana.

What is self-realization? When we become situated in our true nature as the divine soul, it is called 'self-realization'. This is an elevated state of consciousness. The Bhagavad Gita describes such a person as *sthita prajña,* or a sage of steady wisdom (verses 2.56–2.58):

> One whose mind remains undisturbed amidst misery, who does not crave pleasure and who is free from attachment, fear, and anger, is called a sage of steady wisdom. One who remains unattached under all

conditions and is neither delighted by good fortune nor dejected by tribulation, he is a sage with perfect knowledge. One who is able to withdraw the senses from their objects, just as a tortoise withdraws its limbs into its shell, is established in divine wisdom.

What is God-realization? It is a stage much higher than self-realization, where the soul becomes situated in union with God. In that supreme state, the soul receives the divine knowledge, love, and bliss of God. Its *sañchit* karmas are burnt away. The bonds of maya are cut asunder, and the soul is eternally united with God.

Self-realization can be achieved by self-effort. However, to reach God-realization, we require divine grace. Such grace can only be attracted through bhakti. The Bhagavad Gita states:

bhaktyā mām abhijānāti yāvān yaśh chāsmi tattvataḥ
tato maṁ tattvato jñātvā viśhate tad-anantaram

(verse 18.55)

'Only by loving devotion to Me does one come to know who I am in Truth. Then, having come to know Me, My devotee enters into full consciousness of Me.'

The goal of jnana yog is self-realization. The jnani repeatedly contemplates: 'I am not my body. I am not my mind. I am not my intellect.' By such contemplation and other practices, the jnani cuts the bodily illusion.

In contrast, **the path of bhakti yog focuses on attaching the mind to God.** The devotee too contemplates, 'I am not my body; I am the soul', just as the jnani does. The difference is that the bhakti yogi do not stop at this; they further contemplate on their eternal relationship with God.

When, finally, they come to know God, they automatically know the self as well, as a fragment of God. Shree Krishna states in the Bhagavad Gita:

jarā-maraṇa-mokṣhāya mām āśhritya yatanti ye
te brahma tadviduḥ kṛitsnam adhyātmaṁ karma chākhilam

(verse 7.29)

'Those who take shelter in Me, striving for liberation from old age and death, come to know Brahman, the individual self, and the entire field of karmic action.'

While jnanis labour strenuously to know the self, bhaktas realize the self with great ease, when they attain God-realization.

6

Suffering and Calamities

PEOPLE DYING IN NATURAL CALAMITIES

Question: Why do people die in large numbers due to pandemics, wars, or natural calamities? Why does God permit this? Is He signalling that time is up for all the souls in that place or can these be attributed to past karmas?

Answer: People residing in a geographical location have a collective karma associated with them. Natural calamities sometimes occur because of the shared karma of a community of people. However, it is not possible for us to correlate specific episodes with specific collective karmas of a community. The Law of Karma is exceedingly complex, while our human intellect is frail. Even in natural calamities, we see that some are miraculously saved.

Apart from the Law of Karma, there can be other reasons why a calamity befalls. Sometimes God directly intervenes to cause upheavals for upliftment of souls. Adversity throws people outside their comfort zone. They are compelled to battle the circumstances by exerting themselves physically, mentally, and emotionally. The consequent struggle results in inner growth.

Calamities force people to seek answers to the bigger questions of life and gain wisdom. They become nodal points in the journey of the soul from its present mortal imperfection towards immortal perfection.

When a natural calamity befalls, many people view it with disbelief. 'If there is a God, then how could this happen?' But we must remember that the material world is not meant to be a place of unmitigated bliss. It is, in fact, a prison of God. It is a place for souls like us who have our backs towards Him. If this world did not have the aspect of suffering to it, there would be no incentive to detach from the material and seek the spiritual.

The scriptures have called this world *duḥkhālayaṁ* (a place of misery) and *aśhāśhvatam* (temporary). As long as we are in this jail of maya, we should not be astonished when we see suffering. It is not a sign that there is no God, on the contrary, it is an aspect of His creation.

The above points can give us an inkling as to why natural calamities befall. But specifics are not for humans to know. There are many mysteries in the Universe that are simply beyond our comprehension. They will remain mysteries until we become God-realized.

Therefore, having a curious intellect is great, but we must realize its limits. Remember that the world is in the hands of its divine

Creator. Hence, it is best to leave the question of who died, and for what reason, to God.

WHY GOOD PEOPLE SUFFER

Question: Why do bad things happen to good people? This shakes our faith in God—whether He is truly just.

Answer: 'Good things' and 'bad things' are subjective terms—relative to a time frame. Consider this example.

You are to board a train to your grandparents' town for the summer vacation. You get held up in traffic and miss the train. This is so disappointing; you had such great plans for the summer. You berate the circumstances, 'Why did bad luck befall me? Why was there a traffic jam today?'

However, a few hours later, you come to know that the train met with a tragic accident. Now your thoughts make a U-turn. You thank God for His mercy that you were stuck in the jam. If not, you would have been one of the unfortunate passengers. ***What appeared to be a bad thing earlier, turned out to be a blessing in disguise.***

So, when we say, 'Bad things are happening to good people', what is the time frame we are looking at? What appears as 'bad' presently may turn out to be 'good' for inner progress.

Then, what is truly a good or a bad thing? In our narrow perspective, we define 'good things' as the attainment of material luxuries. The deprivation of bodily comforts then becomes our idea of 'bad things'. These labels are, in fact, faulty.

A truly 'good thing' is that which results in our inner growth. A truly 'bad thing' is that which leads to the downfall of our eternal soul.

From this perspective, even suffering may sometimes be a blessing in disguise, or a 'good thing'. This is why, Kunti Devi, mother of the Pandavas, asked God to bestow hardships in her life:

vipadaḥ santu naḥ śhaśhvat tatra tatra jagadguro
bhavato darśhanaṁ yat-syād-apunar-bhava-darśhanam

(Bhagavatam 1.8.25)

'I wish mishaps befall me again and again. They will ensure I keep my eyes on You, Oh Shree Krishna! And then, I will no longer have to see the birth and death (I will be liberated from this cycle).'

If, however, we say that material hardship is our definition of a bad thing, then such 'bad things' happen to everyone. As explained in the previous answer, this material world is God's prison. If the soul could be happy in the material world, it would not serve as a place for reformation. A jail is meant to be a dreary place, for it forces us to keep searching. And this search over a continuum of lifetimes finally brings us to the feet of God.

Additionally, if we are in the prison of God, then we are not such 'good people' after all. At best, we may call ourselves 'moderately good people'.

Hence, the statement, 'Why do bad things happen to good

people?' needs to be amended. It should be: 'Why do bad things happen to moderately good people?' The correct answer is: to make us even better people. Swami Vivekananda commented: 'Life is the continuous unfoldment of a being under circumstances tending to press it downwards.'

In a nutshell, we should embrace challenging circumstances and miseries with the correct spiritual perspective. The proper mindset will enable us to shoot ahead on the spiritual flight ahead of us. Finally, we will start seeing the grace of God in all situations, including the apparently adverse ones.

7

Dilemmas and Viewpoints

SIMPLICITY VS CLEVERNESS

Question: In spirituality, we are taught to be simple and trusting. But my experience is that people in the world take advantage of my simplicity. This upsets me, and I am apprehensive about my straightforwardness. Can you please guide me?

Answer: You have correctly observed the paradox. To negotiate the spiritual and the material arenas of work, we must often deploy contradictory principles.

In the material arena, remember that people are under the influence of maya. They are not beyond selfishness, anger, and greed. This makes them inclined to manipulate and exploit us. **Expecting worldly people to be your selfless well-wishers is naïve.** Do not implicitly trust them. It is advisable to always be cautious in your dealings with them.

If ever you get cheated in the world, learn the lesson and file it in your intellect. The episode will equip you to be more cautious in future. At the same time, release the hurt and resentment, remembering that no one is perfect here. In this way, keep your mind free from bitterness, while at the same time not trusting anyone.

The spiritual path, on the other hand, requires us to be sharanagat (surrendered). Without it, we will not get the grace of the Supreme. For samarpan (surrender), we must take a 'leap of faith'. If we are unwilling to do so, we will not succeed. The difference in the spiritual realm is that trust in God and the Guru does not make us vulnerable. They have no self-interest to fulfil from us.

hari harijan ke kārya ko, kāraṇ kachhu na lakhāy
par upakār swabhāv-vaśh, karat kārya jag āy

(*Bhakti Śhatak* verse 57)

'God and the Saints have no other reason behind Their actions. Their sole intention is the welfare of others. For this purpose alone, They come to the world.'

God and God-realized Saints desire nothing from us. **Their only objective is to help us become the best version of ourselves. Hence, we can completely trust Them, like a baby trusts its mother.** In fact, sharanagati (complete surrender) is a pre-requisite to move forward on the spiritual path.

Therefore, keep both principles in mind. In spiritual matters, work on the principle of faith. In worldly dealings, be cautious and do not allow yourself to get cheated.

HUMILITY VS CONFIDENCE

Question: Can we be humble and confident at the same time? And how can we know that we are confident but not arrogant?

Answer: Humility is viewed by modern society as a weakness. Popular culture teaches us to have pride in ourselves. This is why people often ask me, 'Swamiji, how can I become self-confident?'

The question is: what is this 'self' you are talking about?

- Do you view yourself as the body? If so, it is subject to disease, old age, and death. How can you be confident about your body?
- Do you view yourself as your mind? If so, it is full of defects including anger, greed, hatred, and desires, to name a few. How can you be confident of your mind?

In both the above instances, the basis of self-confidence is itself wrong.

The true self is the 'soul', which is eternally a part of God. Recognizing your spiritual identity will enable you to become humble and confident at the same time.

The foundation of humility should be the belief, 'Without God's grace, I am insignificant and powerless.' With this humble attitude, there will be no question of self-esteem being shattered.

Concomitantly, strengthen the belief, 'If He is by my side, I can do anything.' This will give you unflinching confidence in the mercy of God. But be careful not to become arrogant.

Arrogance is very different from confidence. Arrogant people have an overexaggerated self-worth. They are filled with conceit about themselves and their abilities. They say, 'I am so skilful and great. I can do anything.'

When a task is successfully accomplished, arrogant people use the results to boost their prestige. 'Listen! I did this', 'I did that', and so on. On the contrary, confident people offer the results of their work to God. They say:

yatkṛitaṁ yatkariṣhyāmi tatsarvaṁ na mayā kṛitaṁ
tvayā kṛitaṁ tu phalabhuk tvameva madhusūdana

'Whatever I engaged in and was able to accomplish, it was not me, nor could it ever be me. Oh Shree Krishna! You are the doer of my actions, and the fruits of my actions belong to You.'

Arrogance is the consequence of mistaken identity. Veiled by the ego, we identify with our material personality. We take pride in our fleeting possessions—wealth, beauty, and position. Believing ourselves to be all-important, we forget the significance of God.

The remedy is to always recall how minuscule the soul is. A firefly may be proud of its effulgence at night, but when the sun is in the highest meridian during the day, can it be proud any longer? Likewise, we are so tiny before the infinite opulence of God. We may build one house, but Brahma created the entire universe, and Maha Vishnu manifests unlimited universes.

Our very existence is by His mercy. The Upanishads state: *nityo nityānām chetanaśhchetanānām* 'Our soul is eternal, not because of itself, but because the supremely eternal Lord is sitting within, granting it eternality.' Likewise, we are sentient, not by our own energy, but because God seated within is bestowing us sentience. If the Supreme were to leave us for a moment, our personality itself would not remain.

When we keep this knowledge in our mind—and repeatedly contemplate on it—we will develop confidence without arrogance.

DETACHMENT VS ENTHUSIASM

Question: I don't understand how to balance detachment with enthusiasm for any task. If we give up attachments, what will drive us? Are the two concepts not contradictory to each other?

Answer: In spirituality, the concept of detachment is repeatedly emphasized. Hence, the doubt naturally arises whether detachment results in a lack of motivation. To know the answer, it is important to first understand the concept of detachment.

The spiritual science of work instructs us to perform actions to the best of our abilities while remaining detached from the results. The Bhagavad Gita states:

karmaṇy-evādhikāras te mā phaleṣhu kadāchana

(verse 2.47)

'You have a right to perform your prescribed duties, but you are not entitled to the fruits of your actions.'

Shree Krishna clearly explains that **detachment should not be from performing our duties, rather, it should be from results.** Why? Because the results are not for our enjoyment—they are for the enjoyment of God. Hence, if they are not as per our expectations, we should not be emotionally affected. Accept it as the will of God and move on.

In material consciousness, we believe, 'I am the proprietor of everything I possess. It is all meant for my enjoyment.' So, we work hard to earn wealth, fame, and luxuries. Our drive comes from the enthusiasm to become richer, more popular, more powerful, and more beautiful.

Spiritual consciousness, however, is different. In it, we think, 'God is the owner and enjoyer of the world. He has blessed me with the opportunity to love and serve Him. I will work hard, making the most of the privilege bestowed by God and Guru, and please Them through exceptional service.'

In this manner, with a devotional heart, you become even more enthusiastic. Consider the example of Arjun. He was a warrior before hearing the Bhagavad Gita. After receiving divine knowledge, he did not become lackadaisical. Rather, he was the best warrior on the battlefield. Arjun saw his work as a service to Shree Krishna and was inspired to do it to the best of his ability.

To say that you do not need enthusiasm on the spiritual path is not a correct understanding of detachment. You are factually detaching yourself from lower desires and goals. Simultaneously, you are attaching yourself to a higher purpose that has a far greater ability to motivate you. Hence, it is said:

saṅtośhastriṣhu kartavyaḥ svadāre bhojane dhane
triṣhu chaiva na kartavyo'dhyayane japa dānayoḥ

(*Chanakya Niti*, chapter 7)

The verse says that we should remain content in worldly matters, such as spouse, food, and wealth. But when it comes to spiritual matters—japa, charity, and study of scriptures—we should never be satisfied. Always think, 'I have not done enough as yet; I need to go much further.'

Worldly people work with such zeal—day and night—for fleeting material pleasures. In contrast, as spiritual aspirants, we have the opportunity to offer our works to the Supreme. With this positive inspiration, remain ever enthused for bhakti and seva.

POSITIVITY VS FOCUSSING ON OUR FAULTS

Question: Whenever I look at my faults or defects, it helps vanquish pride. But if I think about it often, then I feel despondent and think, 'How can I even get started?' For a few days, I am not even able to concentrate or meditate.

Answer: In life, introspection is always the stepping stone for self-growth. Awareness of our weaknesses keeps us grounded and free from pride. We realize we have a long way to go. But we should use this realization to our benefit, not detriment.

Modesty based on thoughts, such as 'I am an ocean of defects', 'I owe my very existence to Him', 'It is only because of His grace that I am what I am and where I am', and so on is good. It is the sentiment that all bhakti Saints harboured. However, if you then start thinking, 'I am so fallen that I can never attain divine love', then your thought patterns become counterproductive. Such negative thinking is like hitting your own feet with an axe.

Positive thinking means to only bring those thoughts to your mind that are beneficial. Positive people are solution-oriented; they do not merely keep brooding over the problem. Once aware of their faults, they focus on eliminating them. With enhanced zeal, they apply themselves to life-transformational practices.

So, do not allow negative thoughts about your defects to overwhelm you. For this, you will need these two pieces of knowledge.

- **Positive thoughts come from good beliefs.**
- **Good beliefs come from the right knowledge.**

Thus, revise what the sacred texts say about the nature of God. It will help you develop faith that the Supreme Lord is all-merciful. He is ever ready to lift you up from your current state, provided you engage in His devotion. He has stated in the Bhagavad Gita:

api chet su-durāchāro bhajate mām ananya-bhāk
sādhur eva sa mantavyaḥ samyag vyavasito hi saḥ (9.30)
kṣhipraṁ bhavati dharmātmā
śhaśhvach-chhāntiṁ nigachchhati (9.31)

'Even if the vilest sinners worship Me with exclusive devotion, consider them to be righteous because they have made the proper resolve. Quickly they become virtuous and attain lasting peace.'

Use this knowledge from the holy books to develop the right

beliefs. Remember the causation: Negative thinking stems from faulty beliefs, while positive thoughts are the result of correct beliefs.

If your belief is, 'Sinners can never reach God', then naturally you will lose hope of receiving divine grace. However, if your understanding is, 'God is my eternal Father and is waiting for me with open arms', you will be filled with optimism.

So, **let us live with optimism and faith in the grace of God**. At present, we may be fallen, but if we cry out with devotion, He transforms even the most incorrigible sinners into the purest devotees.

Consider the example of the two notorious brothers in the time of Shree Chaitanya Mahaprabhu. These two brothers, Jagai and Madhai, had created fear in the hearts of everyone in their vicinity. People dreaded their rogue behaviour to the extent that no one ever passed by their house. But eventually, when they admitted their faults and surrendered to Chaitanya Mahaprabhu, they were transformed into Vaishnavas. Those who were earlier the biggest sinners became devotees of a high order.

Therefore, we can be humble and hopeful that God will grace us abundantly.

8

Relationship Skills

FAMILY DOES NOT APPROVE OF BHAKTI

Question: How do I deal with family members who are not aligned with my spiritual choices, which has become a topic of disagreement and contention in the household?

Answer: Spiritual awakening is uncommon. Therefore, do not expect family members or even friends to accompany you, or to support you, on this journey. Learn how to deal with discord in this matter. Here are some pointers that can help you pursue your devotion, while keeping your family members happy.

Reflect on your family members' perspective. Often, your loved ones oppose you as they fear the changes that might happen in their lives due to your devotion. Hence, it becomes imperative to assuage their worries by communicating effectively.

Assure them that you will continue to love them. The truth is that God is our only eternal Relative, while worldly relationships are temporary. However, you do not have to offend your family members by announcing, 'I have no material attachments left. Now, I love God alone.' Such statements will disrupt the family atmosphere and create more hurdles on your path. Instead, be more tactful.

Naturally, as you progress in devotion, your emotional affiliations will change from the material to the spiritual. But it is best not to divulge these changes to your father, mother, spouse, and children. In fact, shower even more affection than before. Set aside some time for your family, and they will be happy.

Explain why devotion is important, but do not argue. Although it feels impossible to convince others about the significance of spirituality, give it a try without losing your temper. Stay calm and collected while discussing your spiritual aspirations and beliefs. Any time the conversations tend to turn towards personal attacks and staunch disagreements, stop the discussion and walk away as Saint Kabir instructed:

hīrā tahān na kholiye, jahān kuṅjaḍon kī hāṭ
bāndho chup kī poṭarī, lāgahu apanī bāṭ

'Do not display your diamonds in a vegetable market. Tie them in a bundle and keeping them in your heart, go on your way.'

When your attempts to share your knowledge are not productive, do not be troubled or angry. This impedes your progress, so guard your knowledge and sadhana carefully.

Words are powerful, but actions speak volumes. Adverse circumstances give us the chance to practise tolerance and compassion towards those who are not yet blessed to tread on this path.

As you display the blossoming of empathy and inner peace, your family members will be inspired to mirror you. I have seen many families in satsang, where one family member embarks on the spiritual path and others soon follow.

Bear in mind that people change. Ratnakar transformed into Valmiki, a God-realized saint who composed the Ramayan even before it actually transpired. The family member who may have been the most vocal about your spiritual aspirations could have a change of heart. They may even overtake you on the spiritual journey.

Grace will come their way in its own time. Meanwhile, you respond to them kindly and continue your sadhana enthusiastically.

DEVELOPING TRUE LOVE

Question: What is true love?

Answer: We all yearn for the euphoric experience of true love. We seek that perfect partner who will love us unconditionally and on whom we can pour our affection, without the fear of being judged or rejected. In short, we all desire love that is authentic and selfless.

However, the love we get in the world comes with the appended baggage of misery and frustration. The heart remains dissatisfied. Five times in a day, lovers change their decision about each other. For instance, a husband thinks: ‘My wife is wonderful’,

'No, she is merely good', 'Well, actually she is just normal', 'In fact, my wife is bad', 'No, she is awful!', and so on.

How come this man's opinion about his wife is varying so much? It is simply selfishness. When he feels that she is fulfilling his self-interest, she is good. When he perceives that she is not giving him happiness but not harming him either, then she is normal. And when he thinks she is harming his self-interest, then she is bad.

See how sentiments towards our loved ones keep seesawing—going up and coming down. It means what we assume to be love is not genuine love. Then, what is real love?

Though 'love' is loosely used to describe feelings in intimate relationships, it has a much more profound meaning. Understand the difference between these three—love, business, and lust.

Lust is dominated by the sentiment of self-pleasure. The mindset is 'take...take...take...' It is as far from love as light is from darkness.

Business involves a give-and-take mindset. 'I did this for you. You must now do this for me, else I do not care about you.'

Love is a deep and noble affection for others' happiness, without seeking personal benefit in return. It is unconditional and selfless.

If your love is genuine, it remains unaffected even when your beloved behaves adversely. True love is when your beloved has been hurtful, yet you continue to love. It does not demand anything and is willing to overlook the other's defects.

The *Ujjwal Neelmani* defines love very aptly:

sarvathā dhvaṅsa rahitaṁ satyapi dhvaṅsa kāraṇe
yadbhāva bandhanaṁ yūnoḥ sa premā parikīrtitaḥ

(verse 14.63)

'Where there is ample reason for love to be devastated, and yet it continues unabated, that is true love.' Here is an inspiring story about such love.

A man married a beautiful girl. They loved each other very much and the marriage proceeded very well. But soon things changed. The wife developed a skin disease, and her complexion began to turn pale. Around that time, the husband left for a tour, where he met with an accident and lost his eyesight.

On his return, the wife took complete care of him. She would hold his hand and help him around the home. Since he was blind, he was unaware that her beauty was fading rapidly. Then the day came when she died. This brought him great sorrow. He finished all her last rites.

As he was about to return from the cremation ground, a friend asked, 'How will you walk by yourself? All these days your wife used to help you.'

He replied, 'I am not blind; I was only pretending because I did not want her to know I was aware of her ugliness.'

Such is the nature of real love; it is causeless and exists for its own sake. It is free from expectations. It is willing to be blind to the other's faults. That is because its goal is not to extract happiness from the other, but instead, to serve.

Finally, to truly love, we must harbour a service attitude, where we look to give to the other, rather than take from them. This was the kind of love the gopis of Vrindavan had for the Lord. Sage Narad describes their love as *tat sukh sukhitvam*. Each thought and action of the gopis was purely for the happiness of their Beloved, Shree Krishna. It was imbued with self-sacrifice and the sentiment of service.

DO I HAVE A SOULMATE?

Question: Most people dream of finding a soulmate as their life partner. However, when I observe relationships in this world, they are always lacking and beset with problems. It makes me wonder: is there any perfect companion or a soulmate at all?

Answer: When we think of a soulmate, we envision someone who is meant to be with us for our entire life. Someone who looks out for our happiness. Someone who will remain with us through life's thick and thin. The problem, however, is in finding such a perfect partner. Why is this so difficult?

All relationships are prone to conflict. The *Merriam-Webster* dictionary defines a soulmate as 'a person who is perfectly suited to another in temperament'. As nice as it sounds, it never happens in the world because no two people's temperaments match completely and at all times.

The disposition of both partners oscillates amongst the three gunas throughout the day. And the moment temperaments differ, friction ensues. This is the reason for conflicts in opinions amongst friends, spouses, parents and children, siblings, business partners, etc.

Worldly relationships are based on self-seeking. We discussed this in the previous question. Each person desires their own happiness from the other.

A boy and a girl came to me and said, 'Swamiji, please give us your blessings. We have decided to get married.'

I called the boy aside and asked, 'Why do you wish to marry this girl?'

'She is very beautiful,' he responded. 'Her father is rich, and she loves me very much. I will get great happiness from her.'

Then I called the girl aside, and asked, 'Why do you wish to marry this boy?'

'He has a very promising corporate career,' she replied. 'He is very handsome and takes great care of me.'

I then got them both together and said, 'Look, both of you wish to marry the other for your own happiness. The moment your self-interest decreases, love will reduce. Hence, this marriage will always remain vulnerable. If you wish to strengthen it, learn to be more selfless.'

Self-seeking is the motivating factor in relationships. 'What can the other do for me?' This is the thought behind our love for others and their love for us. People may say wonderful things: 'You are my *pran priyatam* (dearer than my life).' However, these words do not hold much weight. Consider this humorous incident.

Two lovers were sitting on a park bench expressing that the other was their pran priyatam. A passer-by decided to play a prank and threw a rubber snake between them. Startled, both ran in opposite directions to save their life, unconcerned for the life of the other.

This is the nature of the world. People may claim their readiness to die for you. Yet, foremost, they love their own body and life.

Worldly relationships are temporary. They will cease upon death. We had a different set of relatives in our past lives but have no recollection of them now. Similarly, relatives from the present life will also leave us one day. They will continue into the afterlife according to their karmas.

For all these reasons, there is no such thing as a 'soulmate' in the material realm. But do not be disheartened. Our true soulmate does exist. And who is that? The word for relative in Sanskrit is 'sambandhi'. It refers to that personality with whom we have a 'complete and eternal relationship'.

Such a relative is God. He is seated in our heart and accompanies us from lifetime to lifetime. Since we are His little fragments, our every relationship is with Him. The Bhagavad Gita states:

gatir bhartā prabhuḥ sākṣhī nivāsaḥ śharaṇaṁ suhṛit
prabhavaḥ pralayaḥ sthānaṁ nidhānaṁ bījam avyayam

(verse 9.18)

'I am the Supreme Goal of all living beings, and I am also their Sustainer, Master, Witness, Abode, Shelter, and Friend. I am the

Origin, End, and Resting Place of creation; I am the Repository and Eternal Seed.'

From the platform of the soul, God alone is our soulmate. In Him, we will find true divine love that is infinite in extent, permanent, and ever-fresh, which will forever satiate our soul.

9

Science and Spirituality

SCIENCE VS SPIRITUALITY

Question: Science is based on logic, while spirituality is based on beliefs. For scientific minds, it becomes difficult to accept spirituality. How do we reconcile the two?

Answer: Scientists are trained to understand the world using their material senses. In contrast, spiritual topics require faith in sacred texts, scriptures, and one's Guru. This becomes untenable to scientists, and consequently, science does not give credence to spirituality, making the two disciplines appear as extremes.

However, it does not have to be this way. They are both bona fide branches of knowledge. To harmonize and blend them, let us first explore the common ground.

Both science and spirituality require assumptions. Scientists do not realize that scientific knowledge is also based on the foundation of hypotheses.

For instance, Newtonian mechanics was developed on the assumptions of Euclidean geometry. Then, along came a mathematician called Lobachevsky. He relooked at Euclid's fifth postulate, which states: 'Given a line and a point, only one parallel line can be drawn through that point.' In its place, Lobachevsky postulated: 'Given a line and a point, two or more parallel lines can be drawn through that point.' With this assumption, he developed Lobachevskian geometry. Einstein, in his theory of relativity, utilized Lobachevskian geometry.

We thus see that even science starts off with postulates merely assumed to be true. The assumptions are unproven and could as well be false. In fact, many scientific beliefs of yesteryear have been discredited by later theories. So, when we are willing to work with hypotheses in science, then why such reluctance in taking a leap of faith in spirituality?

Now, coming to the utility of each of these fields, let us appreciate the need for both these branches of knowledge.

Science does not have the solution for all problems. Materialists often view spiritual science as a waste of time and an impediment to economic progress. This, though, is a naïve viewpoint. Without recourse to spiritual techniques, science does not have the capability for eliminating the negative propensities of the mind. We may harness external nature through modern technology, but how will we subdue the forces of our internal nature, such as lust, anger, and greed?

It is also popularly known that one of sins in the list of 'Seven Social Sins' is 'Science without Humanity'[3]. The greatest

[3]'Seven Deadly Sins: As Per Mahatma Gandhi', *Bombay Sarvodaya Mandal & Gandhi Research Foundation,* https://www.mkgandhi.org/mgmnt.htm. Accessed on 22 August 2023.

scientist of the last century, Albert Einstein, put it so well when he said: 'It is easier to denature plutonium than to denature the evil spirit of man.'

He confessed that despite the tremendous advancement of scientific understanding, it still does not possess the expertise for purifying the human mind—that is the realm of spiritual science. To learn the science of mind management, scientists must turn to sacred wisdom.

Besides, science does not have values. It puts nuclear power in our hands, but cannot define good and bad use of that power. Hence, genetic engineering, stem cell technology, and nuclear power have created huge ethical dilemmas that we seem unable to cope with. The resolution of these requires spiritual perspicacity.

Spirituality is also incomplete without science. Some spiritual practitioners proclaim that since we are the soul, we need not pay attention to the body. Simply engage in devotion all day long. However, this viewpoint is equally naïve. If the body falls sick, the mind will be filled with sensations of physical pain. It will then become difficult even to think of God.

Blend both science and spirituality in your life. Consider the two aspects of your personality—the body and the mind. The body must be kept in good shape through material science, while the mind must be cleansed through spiritual science.

The Vedas inform us that there is no conflict between science and spirituality. The *Muṇḍakopaniṣhad* states:

dve vidye veditavye...parā chaivāparā cha (1.1.4)

'There are two kinds of knowledge that we must cultivate—material knowledge and spiritual knowledge.'

Material science helps us understand external nature and harness it for our physical comforts. Spiritual science helps us understand our inner nature and manifest the divinity of the soul within.

In conclusion, if spiritualists say material science is useless, they are wrong. Likewise, if materialists say spirituality is useless, they are also wrong. Just like a train runs on two tracks, we need to utilize both these sciences in our life as well. We will achieve the goal of our life not by rejecting either of these two bodies of knowledge, but by harmonizing and integrating them into our daily life.

SPIRITUALITY VS RELIGION

Question: Swamiji, is it wrong if I am spiritual but not religious? One of the saints in India commented that religion and spirituality are different, but both are necessary. Do you share the same view? What would be your advice to seekers?

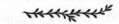

Answer: People commonly use the terms 'religion' and 'spirituality' to describe their beliefs and practices for connecting with sacred principles in their lives. These words are often employed interchangeably. In recent times, however, there is a divergence in how people comprehend the two terms. I will explain here the difference between being religious and being spiritual as per the modern usage of these terms.

Every religion of the world has two dimensions—its religious aspect and its spiritual principles. What does each encompass?

The religious part encompasses procedures for worship, including customs, rituals, and practices. The other, the spiritual part, is its very life. Spirituality is about one's inward journey to purify the mind, cultivate noble virtues, and increase love for God.

For example, in the Hindu tradition, if you visit the four dhams (major holy sites), you are being religious. But if you undertake an inner journey within yourself, you are being spiritual. If you recite prayers from a book, you are being religious. But if you develop a prayerful heart, you are being spiritual. If you wear tilak marks and rosary beads, you are being religious. But if you decorate your heart with ornaments of good virtues, you are being spiritual.

There is no doubt that between the two, spirituality is the essential one. Religiosity will please society and make you look good. Spirituality will please God and make you a better person. This is why all the great prophets and saints inspired people to practise spirituality and develop love for God. Goswami Tulsidas says in verse 6.61.1 of the *Ramcharitmanas:*

milahi na raghupati binu anurāgā, kiyeñ jog, tap gyān birāgā

'Though you may practise yoga, austerities, cultivate bookish knowledge, or display external renunciation, without love and devotion, you will not attain God.'

All the bhakti Saints who came to India during the bhakti era, about 500 years ago, inspired the masses to follow the path of devotion. Their main message was to learn to love God.

The same message is emphasized in other religious traditions as well. When Jesus entered Jerusalem, he chided the scribes and Pharisees—the religious elite of that time. He told them they were performing religious acts but had no love in their hearts. 'These people honour me with their lips, but their hearts are far from me.' (Matthew 15:8)

Thus, our goal is to practise spirituality and develop love for God. But this does not mean we should deride the ritualistic practices of society. Various forms of religious practices are also necessary to create traditions that can be passed down through generations. Most families have a tradition of celebrating religious festivals together. They perform poojas and make offerings to God. These tangible religious acts keep culture alive and bring communities together.

Moreover, religious rituals serve another important purpose. The percentage of people who are truly interested in inner growth is very small. The vast majority do not see the relevance of spirituality to their life. Or if they do, its practices of meditation and contemplation are too subtle for them to connect with. For such people, religious traditions provide tangible practices to engage in.

For example, if people are told to meditate on the Divine, how many will be able to do it? But when asked to do aarti, it becomes feasible. The rituals are easily graspable. That is why 80 per cent of the Vedas propound *karm kand*—the rites and ceremonies. Devotion is described by only 16 per cent of the Vedas—this is the *upasana kand* (devotional section). And *jnana kand* (knowledge section) comprises only 4 per cent of the Vedic mantras.

Hence, religious ceremonies play an important role in human society. They provide a vehicle for gradual spiritual elevation. But once a person has attained a certain level of devotion, the personal importance of religious rituals diminishes. This is because one's mind is naturally engaged in loving devotion, which is the goal of all rituals.

Still, there is no harm in using minimal rituals as aids for bhakti. If offering flowers, water, or food to Shree Krishna enhances your loving sentiments, by all means, continue doing so. But remember that the goal is to perfect our love for God and not the physical act of worship. This way, you can keep a healthy balance between religion and spirituality.

EVIDENCE OF THE SOUL

Question: What is the evidence of the soul? Science does not accept its existence because of lack of proof.

Answer: When it comes to matters of the soul, scientific inquiry has limitations. The instruments of science are material, while the soul is divine. As a result, it does not get perceived in laboratory experiments.

The *Kaṭhopaniṣhad* says:

indriyebhyaḥ parā hyarthā arthebhyaśhcha paraṁ manaḥ
manasastu parā buddhirbhuddherātmā mahān paraḥ

(1.3.10)

'Beyond the senses are the sense objects; even subtler is the mind. Beyond the mind is the intellect; and subtler than all of them is the soul.' This is the reason why we cannot perceive the soul with our senses.

As a crude comparison, suppose an engineer tries to figure out what moves a car. He traces the motion backwards from the wheels to the axle rod, to the gearbox, to the piston. He finally concludes that motion is happening due to the ignition switch, the accelerator, and the steering wheel. He has analysed the machinery correctly but missed the main point: behind all the hardware is the driver who operates it.

Likewise, when doctors look at the functioning of the body, they conclude the brain, heart, and other organs in unison are making it work. They do not perceive that the soul is energizing all these. Nevertheless, there are other ways of knowing that the soul exists. One of these is logical deduction.

The soul's biggest evidence is the existence of free will. We all are aware that we can choose our thoughts and actions. This means we possess a free will. Science, though, has no explanation for the existence of free will.

If, as science postulates, humans are merely an amalgamation of matter, then there is no scope for free will. Just as a computer does not possess the freedom to choose, it functions as per its programmed templates. Likewise, if we are merely the combination of atoms and molecules in the form of the body, then we too should be like pre-programmed machines.

Yet even scientists realize they do have the freedom to choose their beliefs, attitudes, and actions. Existence of the 'self' beyond matter provides the only satisfactory explanation for free will.

Consciousness is the symptom of the soul. At present, science cannot logically explain the presence of consciousness in the body. The prevailing scientific assumption is that life is the result of molecules coming together as the human body. This explanation, however, is not satisfactory because, individually, molecules are devoid of consciousness.

Scientists agree that molecules do not possess a consciousness of their own accord. But they claim that when molecules combine in a particular way, consciousness gets created. Do note that this is simply a hypothesis. It has not been proven experimentally.

The epistemology of science demands proof for everything. So, let scientists also prove their hypothesis by creating life from molecules in the laboratory. And if they cannot validate it experimentally, then why should we accept their theory?

Again, scientists say they are unable to create life from molecules today, but in future, when science advances sufficiently, they will succeed. This is, however, like giving a post-dated cheque and saying, 'I do not have money today, but after 50 years, I will. So please give me your goods.'

Material pleasures do not satiate us. If we are material beings, we should find fulfilment in worldly objects. But even after enjoying material pleasures repeatedly, the feeling of unfulfilment remains. The reason is that our soul is a non-material fragment of God. Our divine nature compels us to seek divine happiness, which is infinite, everlasting, and ever-growing.

Go beyond logic to know the divine soul. Ultimately, God and the soul are beyond material logic since they are divine. Logic can point us towards the existence of the soul but cannot conclusively prove it. Shree Krishna states in the Bhagavad Gita that people cannot understand the soul even after hearing about it.

āśhcharya-vat paśhyati kaśhchid enan
āśhcharya-vad vadati tathaiva chānyaḥ
āśhcharya-vach chainam anyaḥ śhṛiṇoti
śhrutvāpyenaṁ veda na chaiva kaśhchit (verse 2.29)

'Some see the soul as amazing, some describe it as amazing, and some hear of the soul as amazing, while others, even on hearing, cannot understand it at all.'

Apply the scientific process to experience your soul's nature. Even in science, we begin with a hypothesis and then conduct experiments. The results prove or disprove the hypothesis.

Likewise, assume the existence of the soul based on the statement of the scriptures. Now, begin your spiritual practice to purify your mind. As you progress, you will get direct perception of the soul. Shree Krishna has assured in the Bhagavad Gita that through the practice of yog, you will be able to behold the soul:

yatroparamate chittaṁ niruddhaṁ yoga-sevayā
yatra chaivātmanātmānaṁ paśhyann ātmani tuṣhyati
(verse 6.20)

'When the mind, restrained from material activities, becomes still by the practice of yog, then the yogi is able to behold the soul through the purified mind, and he rejoices in the inner joy.'

Until we reach that point of direct perception, we can utilize the above arguments to convince our intellect of the entity called the 'soul'.

10

Jnana—Spiritual Knowledge

HOW TO READ THE SCRIPTURES

Question: Many people memorize the entire Gita. Is this helpful in devotion?

Answer: Whether it is the Bhagavad Gita, Ramayan, or any other scripture, the goal should not be merely *parāyaṇ* (recitation) of the sacred text from start to end. But more importantly, its *ācharaṇ* (implementation) should be our goal.

During his famous dialogue with the yaksha (semi-celestial being) in the well, Yudhishthir said:

pāṭhakāḥ pāṭhakāśhchaiva ye chānye śhāstra chintakāḥ
sarve vyasanino mūrkhāḥ yaḥ kriyāvān sa paṇḍitaḥ

(Mahabharat)

'Those who read the scriptures, those who teach them, and those who philosophize their tenets—they all are foolish dabblers. Only the one who puts their wisdom into practice is the wise pandit.'

So, the best way to read the Gita is slowly—one verse at a time. Look at the verse again. Contemplate deeply on the wisdom. Once it is internalized, try implementing it in your everyday life. This way you will assimilate the knowledge.

Solely memorizing and mindlessly repeating the verses will not take you far. Such mindless repetition is called *tota ratat jnana,* or parrot-like wisdom.

A parrot was taught by its trainer to recite: 'Oh parrot, do not sit on a hunter's net. He will capture you and take you away.' When the trainer saw that his parrot could recite the words, he decided it had become wise and would now be able to fend for itself.

The trainer then released the parrot. The feathered creature flew hither and thither and got caught in a hunter's net. Entangled, it squawked repeatedly, 'Oh parrot, do not sit on a hunter's net. He will capture you and take you away.'

The parrot had memorized the words but had no realization of their meaning. Memorizing the Bhagavad Gita without comprehending its purport can even be dangerous. It can spark false pride. This is called *jnana abhimān,* or the 'conceit of knowledge'. If *jnana abhimān* arises, your study of the scriptures will become counterproductive.

However, if along with memorization, you also assimilate the meaning of the verses, then such knowledge becomes a huge asset in bhakti. Committing verses to memory is a great way of keeping divine wisdom with us because it becomes easy to recall the knowledge whenever needed. So, by all means, do commit the verses to memory but remember their ultimate purpose. Saint Kabir states:

padane kī had samajh hai, samajhan kī had gyan
gyan kī had hari nām hai, prem nām had jān

'The outcome of reading should be understanding. True understanding results in wisdom. The culmination of wisdom is faith in the divine Name. Repeated remembering of God's Name should lead to divine love, which is the ultimate goal of the spiritual journey.'

With that in mind, study the scriptures so you understand them. Then, with firm faith, implement the knowledge in your life. And finally, cultivate love for God in your heart.

RETAINING KNOWLEDGE

Question: I get inspired by the spiritual wisdom you share when I hear it. However, I forget many of the points you make after a few days. How can we retain that knowledge all the time?

Answer: We naturally feel inspired when we hear divine wisdom. But with time, our motivation wanes. The reason is that learning has the tendency to slip out of our intellect with the passage of time. For knowledge to continue to be useful, it must stay in our active recollection, as the following story illustrates.

There was a beautiful young apsara (celestial maiden). She had been cursed that if the person she married ever saw his reflection, he would turn into a frog. Many handsome suitors were attracted by the apsara's beauty and would propose to marry her. But when she informed them of the curse, they would change their mind.

One day, a king saw her and got enchanted. He asked for her hand in marriage. She told him of the curse as well. 'It is not a problem,' responded the king. 'I am a powerful monarch and will get all reflective surfaces removed from my kingdom.'

Reassured, she married him. A few joyous years went by. Then, one day the king went out hunting and lost his way. Hungry and thirsty, he came to the edge of a lake. As he stooped to drink its water, he forgot the curse and saw his reflection in the pond. Immediately, he turned into a frog.

The moral of the story is that when knowledge is forgotten, it becomes futile. The Vedas state: *tattva vismaraṇāt bhekivat* 'If you forget *vivek* (discernment), you will become like a beast.' To be truly human requires steadfast awareness of wisdom and its utilization for discriminating the right from the wrong.

Hence, merely hearing good knowledge does not suffice. We must preserve it and then implement it when situations arise. Here is the three-step process to do this.

***Śhravaṇ* (hearing).** The first step is to spend time reading or hearing divine knowledge. Enrich your intellect by soaking in wisdom from the Vedic scriptures and your Guru.

In this matter, people become complacent. They say, 'We have already heard our Guru's lecture. There is no need to hear it again.' A single hearing, however, does not suffice. We are not in the category of Arjun, who heard the Bhagavad Gita just once, and said: *nașhțo mohaḥ smṛitir labdhā* 'Oh Shree Krishna! My ignorance is gone, and I am now seated in knowledge.'

In our case, our material intellect is so defective that even great ascetics and sages admit defeat before it. So, we must hear good knowledge again and again. The Brahma Sutra states: *āvṛitti rasa kṛitupadeśhāt* 'Repeatedly hear the divine teachings to reinforce the concepts.'

***Manan* (contemplation).** After hearing, the next step is to think deeply about it. This is also called chintan. It helps in getting the knowledge to stick to our intellect. For that, take one gem of wisdom and mull over it like a cow chewing cud for hours to aid digestion. Even one nugget of knowledge, if sufficiently reflected upon, has immense transformative power.

***Nididhyāsan* (firm belief).** The final step is to create a belief in accordance with the knowledge. It will happen when the intellect firmly decides 'this is it'. Through *nidhidhyāsan*, we transform scriptural tenets into empowering beliefs. This step is most important and will make a big difference. The *Kaṭhopaniṣhad* explains the power of beliefs in this mantra:

astīstyevopalabdhasya tattvabhāvaḥ prasīdati (2.3.13)

Though we all intuitively know the definition of God, our intellect does not believe it. Hence, our knowledge—that He is all-powerful, all-pervading and all-knowing—is merely theoretical. The mantra states that if we simply believe in this definition, we will become God-realized. There is nothing further to be done.

This is the power of good beliefs. And what is the way to develop them? It is the three-step formula we have just discussed:

hearing-contemplation-faith or *śhravaṇ-manan-nididhyāsan*.

Compare knowledge with water. When water is heated and made to boil at 100 degrees celsius, it transforms into steam. The steam is then pressurized and used for driving turbines to generate electricity. But if you heat water to 99 degrees celsius, it will remain liquid and cannot drive the turbines.

Likewise, until knowledge is retained and acted upon, it remains powerless. But when assimilated and implemented, it transforms into powerful wisdom. It now changes the trajectory of your life.

11

Bhakti—Devotional Practices

EKADASHI FASTING

Question: What is the significance of fasting on Ekadashi? It has strict guidelines. Certain foods such as grains are not permitted. Only homemade food is to be eaten. It becomes difficult to adhere to such stringent rules in modern times. Should we follow these guidelines? What is your advice regarding fasting, Swamiji?

Answer: Fasting is a common practice across many religions. In Hindi and Sanskrit, the word used for fasting is *upavās*. Etymologically, *vās* means 'to sit', while *up* means 'close to God'. Fasting is thus a way of bringing yourself close to God. The goal is that on the day of the fast, you think less about food and instead, engage the mind in devotion.

Now, what is special about an Ekadashi fast? It falls on the eleventh day of the waxing and waning moon. Thus, Ekadashi comes twice a month, or once every fortnight. It is a widely observed fast among Vaishnavas (followers of Bhagavan

Vishnu). And yes, there are strict guidelines advocated for this fast.

In North India, people do not eat wheat on this day. They believe *pāp purush* (sin personified) resides in wheat on that day. So, they are fine with eating rice. In South India, the opposite is practised. They do not eat rice on this special day, as they believe sin resides in rice, but wheat is okay. Others omit grains altogether but take alternate food items that do not contain grains. These can include kuttu atta puri, rajgiri halwa, and milk products, such as kalakand and rasgullas. The fast then turns into a feast!

In this manner, the way it is presently being practised, the fast has become more about the rituals tied to it, and the bhakti element has been forgotten. Focussing solely on abstaining from eating certain foods defeats the very purpose of fasting.

In another vein, if one desists from food, but constantly thinks, 'When will the day end? When will Dwadashi come (the day after Ekadashi, when the fast is broken)?', the mind has gone more closer to food than on normal days. The goal of the fast—which was to remember God—is lost. We have simply clasped the ritual and made a sham of it. It would have been better to eat food as on other regular days, and instead, just increase the time spent in devotion. That would have been the real *upavās*—taking the mind closer to God.

All the saints and scriptures teach love for God. To help us in our devotion, they also prescribe some rituals. But human nature is such that we forget the devotional part and make a big deal about the rules of the ritual. We must therefore remind ourselves that the goal is to increase our love for God, on Ekadashi, Dwadashi, and every day.

ASKING GOD FOR A BOON

Question: Why is it wrong to ask God for material boons? Is it okay to ask Hari and Guru to eradicate material setbacks that are hindering our spiritual progress? I want to do sadhana early in the morning, but I am unable to wake up despite many attempts. Can I ask God for help in this regard?

Answer: The Almighty, all-merciful God is our true well-wisher. As His little children, we turn to Him to get our desires fulfilled. Some beg him for a job, others for their child's health, yet others for wealth. But this is not true devotion. Sage Narad states in his *Bhakti Darshan*: *sā na kāmayamānā nirodh rūpatvāt* 'Bhakti should not be tainted by prayers for the fulfilment of selfish desires.'

What are the drawbacks of asking God for material boons? First, God is not a waiter that we ring a bell and He responds to our command. He has laws in place by which He administers the world. One of these is the Law of Karma. It states that whatever one does, one reaps the results accordingly.

Now, when we ask God for material blessings, what do we do? For example, we say, 'Oh Hanumanji! I will offer You five kilograms of laddus. Please do this work of mine.' We are, in effect, hoping to bribe Hanumanji with laddus and expecting

Him to waive the Law of Karma for us. Do you think it will work?

Hanumanji is a divine personality. He will not bend the Law of Karma for 5 or 500 kilograms of laddus. But, suppose by our own deeds, our desire gets fulfilled, then what will happen? Our faith will increase. We will say, 'Hanumanji is so kind. He did this for me.'

The problem with such faith is that it is not stable because there is never an end to desires. Next time we have a need, we will again say, 'Oh Hanumanji! Yesterday, You did that for me; today, please do this.'

Now, suppose this time, by our own karmas, our desire is not fulfilled. What will happen? Our faith—that had gone up—will come crashing down. We will say things like, 'Hanumanji does not listen. How hard-hearted He is.'

In this way, our shraddha (faith) will fluctuate from day to day. It is also possible that one day we may turn around from God and become an atheist. There are so many in the world who say, 'God did not take care of me, so I no longer believe in Him.' Their own incorrect expectation from God turned them against Him.

The bigger problem with this kind of 'sakaam bhakti' (selfishly motivated devotion) is that our mind does not get purified. Instead of focussing on God, our mind stays entangled in worldly desires.

Let us say, for example, you visit a doctor and request him to cure your ailing son. Are you engaging in devotion towards the doctor? Definitely not! Your mind is attached to your son; the doctor is the medium for curing him. Likewise, if we go to God with material desires, our mind remains in the desires, so cleansing does not happen.

That is why, if you seek to purify your heart, firmly resolve not to ask the Lord for material boons.

Now, coming to the second part of your question—should you ask God to remove obstacles in the way of devotion?

Let us first understand the nature of nishkaam bhakti (selfless devotion). In it, we do not seek our own happiness but the happiness of God.

Once you establish your goal as nishkaam bhakti, you can definitely ask Him for the ability to serve Him. It will still be considered nishkaam (selfless), since the intention behind your request is His pleasure.

So, **you can selflessly seek God's help in overcoming a barrier to your devotion.** Remember not to demand that He make your situation more comfortable for you. Instead, make your prayer something like this:

'Oh Shree Krishna! I wish to serve You with all my heart. But due to my material infirmities, I fall short. Please bestow on me the faith, devotion, and self-control, that I may serve You well. If You wish to remove obstacles I face in bhakti, it is up to You. Whatever be the case, I will continue putting all my best efforts in loving service to You.'

The beauty of this selfless prayer is that we are leaving the outcome to God's will. He will then decide what is best for us and bestow the highest thing. As the saying goes: *bin māñge motī mile, māñge mile na bhīkh* 'By selfish entreaties, you get nothing. But when you become selfless, He gives you everything.'

We remained a beggar before God for so many lives. Let us now decide that we will not think, 'What can God do for me?' Instead, we will focus on what we can give to Him. And in the process, we will receive the biggest treasure, which is para bhakti (divine love).

SPIRITUAL REWARDS FROM RITUALS

Question: Do rituals, fasts, and bathing in the river Ganga give us spiritual benefits? Do we earn good karma and absolve our sins?

Answer: The Vedic scriptures describe a variety of rites, poojas, and ceremonies. The underlying purpose of all these is explained in the *Padma Puran*:

smartavyaḥ satataṁ viṣhṇur vismartavyo na jātuchit
sarve vidhi-niṣhedhāḥ syur-etayor eva kiṅkarāḥ

(*Bhakti Rasāmrit Sindhu* 1.2.8)

The verse states that all rituals were designed to serve a two-fold purpose: **1) to always remember God, and 2) to never forget Him.**

Unfortunately, over time, people have lost the spiritual essence of these religious ceremonies. They engage in the physical processes with their body, while the mind contemplates worldly things.

For example, when people purchase a new house or a new car, they call a pandit to perform a ceremony. And while the pandit does the pooja, they sit and chit-chat in the other room or sip a cup of tea. For them, devotion is nothing more than the inattentive performance of rituals.

Such ceremonies—devoid of devotion—cannot help us attain the ultimate goal, which is love for God. The Shreemad Bhagavatam states:

dharmaḥ svanuṣṭhitaḥ puṁsāṁ, viṣhvaksena-kathāsu yaḥ
notpādayed yadi ratiṁ, śhrama eva hi kevalam (1.2.8)

'You may perform a ritual in the most perfect manner. But if it does not result in devotion at the lotus feet of God, then it is wasted effort.'

Thus, bathing our body in the holy Ganga is not the end goal. It is a means for nurturing our devotion to the Supreme. However, as we grow in devotion, the physical ritual becomes unimportant. That is because you can now spontaneously take your mind to God without the help of external support. The *Manu Smṛiti* states:

yamo vaivasvato devo yas tava-eṣha hṛidi sthitaḥ
tena ched-avivādas-te mā gaṅgā mā kurūn gamaḥ (8.92)

In this verse, the progenitor Manu states that God is seated in your heart. The day you believe this, there will be no further need for pilgrimage to Ganga or Kurukshetra.

Regarding this, Saint Ravidas' statement is famous: *mana*

chañgā to kaṭhautī me gaṅgā. He says that if our mind is pure, then a pilgrimage to the Ganga is unnecessary. You can accrue the same fruit by contemplating the Ganga in a pot of water. Simply sit at home and meditate.

Here is a sample meditation and prayer that will bestow the benefit of Ganga snan (bath) while sitting in your home itself. Sit with your eyes closed in any meditative posture. Then visualize and think in the following manner:

Maha Vishnu is the Master of infinite material universes. The sacred waters from His lotus feet are flowing into our universe as the holy Ganga. It is purifying the celestial abodes and then descending to the earth.

I am fortunate to be sitting at its bank, receiving the blessings of the Lord through these sacred waters. I offer my prayers to the holy river to carry my humble message to its source. 'Oh Ganga! I have been waiting for God's grace, while you are descending directly from His feet. Please convey my entreaty to Him to fill my heart with loving devotion. I shall be eternally indebted.

Oh Mother Ganga! You are divinely pure, while I have committed endless sins in innumerable past lives. Today, I pray to you to cleanse my body, mind, and intellect, so that I may never ever sin again in future.'

With this meditation, you can bathe your mind in the Ganga, while sitting at home. This is the beauty of spirituality; it is an inner journey related to the purification of our consciousness. While the world pays importance to external acts, God notes the thoughts and intentions in our mind.

There are two styles of doing devotion—*vaidhi* bhakti and *rāgānugā* bhakti. Understand the difference between the two.

In *vaidhi* bhakti, the ritualistic procedures are very elaborate and excessive. Do parikrama (circumambulation) of the Tulsi plant three times. Wear the *kanthi* mala in a particular manner. Chant on the beads for this many rounds. While doing aarti, ring the bell like that. While offering bhog, sprinkle water in this specific manner. The list goes on and on.

In *rāgānugā* bhakti, you neither waste time in cumbersome ceremonies nor do you get entangled in complex rituals. Instead, you directly engage the mind in God. Observe only those rituals that assist you in your devotion. And for the rest, keep the practice internal. Bathe your mind with sacred thoughts and adorn your heart with divine Virtues.

12

Practice of Sadhana

THE NEED FOR DAILY SADHANA

Question: My spiritual battery gets fully charged when I attend the JKYog Weekend Retreats (sadhana camps). But when I return home, I am not able to retain the devotional high. What is an effective technique I can incorporate to stay spiritually charged at home?

Answer: What happens in these three-day spiritual retreats? You are in an environment where there is no worldly disturbance. Your only work is to meditate, contemplate, self-reflect, devote, and pray. All these actions elevate your consciousness to a higher dimension.

On the first day, as you participate in spiritual activities, you experience that the mind has to be gently coaxed to the divine realm. On the second day, the mind seems to flow more naturally to God. The satsang environment and everything around helps. Now, worldly thoughts are few and far between.

Then on the third day, when you wake up in the morning, you find your mind in a state of blissful immersion. By the time the retreat ends, people come and tell me, 'Swamiji, these were the most blissful days of my life.' The reason for the experience of bliss was that the mind became completely absorbed in the Supreme Divine Personality.

Now, when you return home what happens? All day long, you live in a distractive environment. Material activities, people, and conversations—all tend to increase the mind's worldliness. Despite your best intentions, disturbances sweep away your progress and soil your mind again. So, in order to keep your mind elevated at home, you must dedicate some time for secluded sadhana (spiritual practice) on a daily basis.

Consider the example of milk. When mixed with water, it cannot retain its undiluted identity. However, if the milk is kept apart from water, converted into yogurt, and then churned to extract butter, it becomes immiscible. It can now challenge the water, 'I will sit on your head and float. You can do nothing to me now, for I have become butter.'

Similarly, our mind is like milk and the world is like water. In contact with the world, the mind becomes worldly and cannot retain divine consciousness. But an environment of seclusion blocks distraction, making it conducive to focus the mind on God. Once sufficient absorption in the Supreme has been achieved, then we too can challenge the world, and say, 'I will live amidst all the dualities of maya, and yet remain untouched by them.'

This sublime state is reached through sadhana in isolation.

The Bhagavad Gita also emphasizes it in verse 18.52: *vivikta sevī laghv-āśhī* 'Practice sadhana in a secluded place; control your diet.'

Thus, we should allocate some time in our daily schedule for spiritual practice in solitude. Shutting ourselves out from the world, we should practise meditation, contemplation, introspection, and devotion. This will help purify our mind and fill it with divine thoughts and noble aspirations.

HOW SHOULD I SET UP MY DAILY PRACTICE?

Question: I am a beginner in spiritual practices. How do you recommend I set up my daily sadhana?

Answer: Aspirants repeatedly have questions regarding the best time for sadhana, how long it should be done, what direction to face, and so on. Let us address these questions one at a time.

How long should I do sadhana every day? Ideally, you should spend two hours daily, which equates to about one-tenth of your day. However, if this is not practical, commit to at least one hour. But be firm in your resolve to follow this regimen.

What is the best time for sadhana? The early morning hours are the best. They are called *Brahma Muhūrt*, or 'the time for God'. These are the two hours just before sunrise—roughly 4.30–6.30 a.m. They are ideal because you have just woken up and your mind is empty. The environment is serene and free from distractions, making it conducive to readily absorbing the mind in devotion.

We read in the Puranas how the sages, yogis, and rishis of yore were all early risers. Like them, if we too wish to achieve spiritual mastery, we must claim the first portion of our day. However, if this is not possible due to your work schedule, you may allocate any alternative time suitable for you. In setting up your timetable, the principle is to keep in mind your individual need and convenience.

What should be my posture while I sit for sadhana? In bhakti sadhana, posture is not important. You can sit in any comfortable posture. However, in the initial stages, you could easily doze off while meditating. To avoid this, you should sit upright and not take back support from a wall.

Postures such as padmasan (lotus pose), ardh padmasan (half-lotus pose), dhyānvīr asan (hero's meditative pose), siddhasan (accomplished pose), and sukhasan (cross-legged) are all suitable. Maharishi Patanjali, in his *Yog Darshan*, explains: *sthira sukham āsanam* (2.46). He states aptly that to practise meditation, sit in any posture you find easy provided you can sit alert and stationary in it for an extended period of time.

What direction should I face while sitting in sadhana? Just like the posture, the direction is also not important. Every direction is pure and pristine because God is all-pervading in creation. The *Śhwetāśhvatar Upaniṣhad* states:

eko devaḥ sarvabhūteṣhu gūḍhaḥ sarvavyāpī (6.11)

'There is one God. He is seated in everyone's heart. He is also everywhere in the world.' The *Puruṣha Sūktam* states:

puruṣha evedaṁ sarvam yad bhūtaṁ yachcha bhavyam

(verse 2)

'God pervades everything that has existed and all that will exist.'

Hence, the emphasis must be on absorbing the mind in sublime thoughts, not the direction in which we sit. It is, however, beneficial to have a designated corner in your home for devotion. You can set up an altar in this place, with pictures of God and Guru. Over time, the mind begins to associate the spot with bhakti. It falls into the habit of getting into meditation mode whenever you go and sit there.

These are the basic steps to set up your sadhana routine. Once established, you must then incorporate different techniques to absorb your mind in God.

IS KIRTAN COMPULSORY IN SADHANA?

Question: Why is singing of kirtans so popular in India? What are its benefits? Is it compulsory to add singing to bhakti and sadhana?

Answer: Singing kirtans is definitely not compulsory. But first let us understand: What is kirtan? And what are its benefits?

The *Bhakti Rasāmṛit Sindhu* defines kirtan as:

nāma-līlā-guṇadīnām uchchair-bhāṣhā tu kīrtanam (1.2.145)

'Singing the Names, Pastimes, Forms, Abodes, Associates, and Virtues of God is called kirtan.'

Great saints in history composed many bhajans and kirtans. They encouraged the congregational singing of kirtans as a simple yet effective way for engaging people in devotion. Kirtan is a three-fold process of devotion (*tridhā* bhakti) consisting of *śhravaṇ* (hearing), kirtan (chanting), and *smaraṇ* (remembering).

In this three-fold process, most important is *smaraṇ*—remembering God. The reason is that our mind is the cause of bondage and liberation, and the goal of sadhana is to purify it. Hence, if we wish, we can simply **think of or meditate on** Shree Krishna, without singing or hearing. It is perfectly acceptable; there is no compulsion to do kirtans.

Keep in mind that *śhravaṇ* and kirtan can greatly assist *smaraṇ*. This is because they engage our senses in devotion, thereby keeping our thoughts from wandering off. Hence, they serve as helpers to meditation.

The bhajans we sing contain many ingredients for devotion. Often, they are poetic prayers written by God-realized Saints. Singing them is a great way of offering our own prayers and relishing the bhakti *rasa*. We can sing kirtans to cry out to God with all our heart, while shedding tears of loving devotion.

Kirtan has another important benefit. Most people do not have an insulated environment for meditation. Many distracting sounds and noises abound. In kirtan, the melodious ragas block out disturbances from the surroundings, insulating us from diversions.

Kirtan is a good medium for contemplation. Bhajans are filled with the glories of the Names, Abodes, Forms, Virtues, and Pastimes of the Lord. As we hear and sing them, we naturally dwell on the meaning of bhajans. Thus, they become excellent aids for deep reflection.

The Shreemad Bhagavatam extols the virtues of kirtan as a form of sadhana:

kalerdoṣha nidherājannasti hyeko mahān guṇaḥ
kīrtanād eva kriṣhṇasya muktasaṅgaḥ paraṁ vrajet

(12.3.51)

'Kali yug is an ocean of faults, but it has one great quality. By doing kirtan of Shree Krishna, one is easily liberated from maya and attains the divine Abode.'

For all these reasons, kirtan is called the yuga dharma (spiritual practice of the times) in the present age of Kali. Still, we must not forget that mechanical chanting by itself will not purify the mind. Hearing and chanting are only helpers while the essence is remembrance. Always keeping the mind attached to God is of paramount importance. This brings us to the discussion on meditation.

HOW TO MEDITATE

Question: Swamiji, what are the benefits of meditation? I have read and heard about so many schools of meditation that I am quite confused. Please guide me on how to meditate properly.

Answer: Meditation has been around ever since the beginning of humankind. Most of the major religions have had it as a part of their mystical practices. It grew in popularity in the Western world in the eighteenth century when some of the Eastern books of wisdom were translated into European languages. Then, in the 1960s, spiritual teachers from India popularized it in mainstream America. Over time, the practice has expanded from a spiritual technique to a chic trend. Today, it is performed in fitness studios, office meetings, and universities. Airlines even offer in-flight meditation options!

The reason for the growing popularity of meditation is its numerous benefits—physiological, psychological, and spiritual. It reduces the stream of thoughts crowding the mind and brings tranquillity. Through meditation, we can go within our mind and intellect and work upon them, thereby gaining control over our emotions. One of meditation's greatest advantages is its ability to steady the mind and develop the power of focus.

As a spiritual discipline, the goal of meditation is to cleanse the mind by bathing it in noble and sublime thoughts. Ultimately, when practised with faith and devotion, it becomes a means for reaching the Supreme.

This is where most popular meditation techniques fall short. They do bestow tranquillity and focus, but they do not connect the tiny soul with the Supreme Soul. Additionally, since the object of meditation is often material, they do not completely purify the mind.

How do we cleanse the mind through meditation? For this, we must fix our mind on something that is transcendental to the material gunas. Such an all-pure object is God. In the Bhagavad Gita, Shree Krishna states:

māṁ cha yo 'vyabhichāreṇa bhakti-yogena sevate
sa guṇān samatītyaitān brahma-bhūyāya kalpate

(verse 14.26)

'Those who attach their mind to Me rise above the three modes of material nature and come to Me.'

Understanding this simple truth, decide firmly, 'I wish to meditate upon the Supreme and not on mere lights or chakras or anything else.' Once you have this clarity, confusion regarding meditation will cease.

How can we meditate upon God? Our mind is naturally habituated to recalling forms and images of people and events. For example, when we think of our friends, we first remember their form. This is the mind's nature; it is more easily drawn towards images than it is to names.

Similarly, if we endeavour to meditate merely on the syllable 'Om', we will find it difficult to keep our mind focussed. But if we focus on the all-attractive form of God, it will be much easier. This is called 'Roop Dhyan' meditation. When we have the image of our Lord, we get a tangible basis for rapidly growing our love for Him.

How to do 'Roop Dhyan' meditation. This is a very natural and power-packed way of growing your devotion to God. With it, meditation does not feel like hard work; the emotional connect happens and the soul experiences devotional bliss. Here are the steps involved.

1. Visualize the form of your *Iṣhṭa Dev*. You can imagine Him present before you or sitting within your heart. You can even

take yourself mentally to the divine Abode and visualize your *Iṣhṭa Dev* there.

2. Add devotional sentiments to your thoughts. Think of God's divine Qualities, such as His infinite beauty, kindness, and compassion. The more you contemplate on His divine Virtues, the more your love for Him will grow.
3. Sweeten this further by meditating on His Pastimes (leelas). You can envision those described in the scriptures or make up your own leelas. For example, imagine God coming to your home. You are welcoming Him, seating Him in your living room, and doing His aarti.
4. You can take it a step further by doing manasi seva (mental service). Visualize yourself taking care of God, singing for Him, massaging His feet, and so on. This strengthens the richness of your sentiments.

Initially, the mind will wander. In the beginning, as we meditate, despite our best efforts, the mind will go off into the world. Many people get discouraged by this and give up their practice. However, we must not feel despondent. Maharishi Patanjali states:

abhyāsa vairāgyābhyāṁ tannirodhaḥ (*Yog Darshan* 1.12)

'The perturbations of the mind can be controlled by constant practice and detachment.'

Practice is the key. Every time the mind runs into the world, pull it back. This is called *vairāgya* (detachment). Then, bring the mind to rest on God. This is *abhyās* (practice). When trained in this way, the mind will stabilize on the Supreme Divine Personality.

Along with meditation, in your daily sadhana, you should also engage in other spiritual practices. These include self-reflection, contemplation of the scriptures, prayer, and kirtan. Here are some online resources to assist you in your daily sadhana.

KripaluPadhati. The aforementioned disciplines are part of the *KripaluPadhati* format of practising sadhana. You can delve further into these in my book, *The Science of Mind Management*.

To access these tools online, you can visit our website: *https://www.jkyog.org/store/product/kripalu-padhati-kripalu-prakriya-workshop*.

Comprehensive Online Course. JKYog offers an online Vedic philosophy course, *Daily Sadhana*, for your spiritual growth. It provides aspirants with 60 minutes of prayer, kirtans, discourse, and meditation everyday, which they can do at their own pace from the comfort of their home. It can be accessed at *https://www.mydailysadhana.org/*

JKYog Online Classes. You can take advantage of 100+ free online classes every week. They are a great way of acquiring divine wisdom and practical implementation techniques. These can be accessed at *https://www.jkyog.org/online-classes* or at *https://www.jkyog.in/online-sessions/*.

INCREMENTAL PROGRESS IN SPIRITUALITY

Question: In my journey of spirituality, I am struggling to be consistent and apply your teaching of incremental growth.

Where am I going wrong?

Answer: Spiritual practice is a gradual process, requiring patience and perseverance. Unfortunately, in this age of 'instant coffee' and 'two-minute noodles', patience has become a rare virtue.

In spirituality too, people look for quick results. 'Today, I am entangled in vices; tomorrow, I should have no bad habits.' 'Yesterday, I was besieged by negativities. Today, I must be 100 per cent free of evil thoughts.' 'Presently, I am a sinner. Soon, I must become a saint.'

If these ambitious goals are not achieved, people become dejected. Some even leave the path permanently, having concluded they can never succeed. However, success is not an occurrence that happens in one day; it is a journey that is undertaken, one fruitful step at a time.

People make the mistake of overestimating the change they can make in a day. But more importantly, they also underestimate the cumulative effect of daily small changes over time.

A Guruji had his ashram in the Himalayas. One night, he told his disciple, 'There is a Babaji living in the monastery one kilometre away. Meet him and bring him with you.'

The disciple said, 'Guruji, how will I go in the dark?'

Guruji gave him a lantern. The disciple remarked, 'This is throwing light only to a distance of 10 metres, while the Babaji's hut is a kilometre away. How can I use this to travel so far?'

Guruji replied, 'My child! Presently it is enabling you to see 10 metres. So, you can go that far, upon which the lantern will show another 10 metres. In this way, you can keep walking until you reach your destination.'

In the same way, people come to me and say, 'Swamiji, this goal of complete surrender to God is so difficult. I am nowhere near it.' Do not let that discourage you. Instead, focus on how to take the next step.

Let us say, for example, that you are learning to meditate. On the first day, suppose you succeed for just two of the ten minutes. Do not be disappointed. Keep practising. In just a few weeks, you will be successfully meditating for three of the ten minutes. Then four. And when you cross the 50 per cent mark, the progress will speed up exponentially. But you must still continue the practice. Then, one day you will reach perfection. The *Yoga Sutra* states:

sa tu dīrgha-kāla nairantarya-satkārāsevito dṛiḍhabhūmiḥ

(*Samādhi Pāda* 1.14)

'When practice is continued for a long duration with dedication and without interruption, it becomes firmly grounded as a habit.' Little changes over a long period of time lead to big transformations.

What does that mean on the spiritual path? There are no quick fixes—the journey is long and arduous. Instead of feeling demoralized, continue enthusiastically with your practice. Keep your eye on the goal and strive deliberately to improve one delta every day.

With time, your practice will gain momentum. Finally, the

day will arrive when you would have installed the new habits and mindsets you cherish. That is why the *Aitareya Upanishad* states:

charaiveti charaiveti, charan vai madhu vindati

'Keep moving forward. Keep moving forward. The bee that keeps moving, without giving up, gets the honey.'

13

Forms of God

WHICH FORM TO WORSHIP

Question: Growing up, I saw my parents worshipping Ram, Sita, and Hanuman. After marriage, I see my in-laws praying to Radha Krishna. I am now confused as to which God to worship. Please guide me as to what form of God would be most beneficial in my devotion.

Answer: The land of India has been blessed with many Avatars of God. However, these are not different Gods; They are various forms of the same one God. The Vedas clearly state:

ekam-eva-advitīyaṁ bramha
ekaṁ sat viprāḥ bahudhā vadanti
eko hi rudro na dvitīyāya tasthuḥ
ekaṁ santaṁ bahudhā kalpayanti

All these Vedic mantras state that there is only one Supreme Divinity who takes on different Forms.

We too appear differently on a variety of occasions. We have one attire when we are in the office, another when relaxing at home, and a third when at the tennis court. The distinction between God and us is that we do not possess the ability to be in all three places at the same time.

However, God is all-powerful and can exist in numerous Forms at the same time. Therefore, Ram, Krishna, Shiv, Durga, and Narayan are all Forms of the same Supreme Lord.

Now the question arises: should we worship all of them or should we choose one Form to worship? A famous Hindi proverb states:

ek sādha sab sadhe, sab sādhe sab jāy

It means, 'If you focus all your attention on one goal, you will succeed in it. But if you try to succeed in multifarious things simultaneously, you will fail in all.'

Similarly, if you try to love all the Forms of God—one on Monday, another on Tuesday, a third one on Wednesday, and so on—then you will end up developing love for none. Instead, if you consistently contemplate on one, you will eventually develop love for all Forms of the Divine. For rapid progression on the spiritual path, therefore, it is recommended to choose one *Iṣhṭa Dev* (the devotee's chosen form of God).

While choosing your *Iṣhṭa Dev* is a matter of personal preference, here are some points to keep in mind:

Select an enchanting form. If the form of your *Iṣhṭa Dev* is attractive, then it will be easier to attach your mind to Him/Her. From that viewpoint, Shree Krishna has a very charming Form, which greatly facilitates devotion.

Enthral your mind with the divine Pastimes. To engage the mind in God, simply meditating on the Form does not suffice; the leelas also help greatly. If our *Iṣhṭa Dev* displayed nectarous Pastimes, by hearing and remembering them, we can easily absorb our mind in Him. It is for this reason that devotion to Ram and Krishna is the most popular.

Relish the nectar of devotion. Lastly, there is an added advantage in the worship of Shree Krishna. We do not even need to put Him on a pedestal and create distance and formality with Him. We can simply look on Him as our own—we can see Him as our Friend, Child, or even Soul-Beloved. Consequently, the bliss of devotion becomes exceedingly sweeter. To savour such bliss, or *Braj Ras,* the great devotee Uddhav prayed:

āsām aho charaṇa-reṇu-juṣhām ahaṁ syāṁ
vṛindāvane kim api gulma-latauṣhadhīnām

(Shreemad Bhagavatam 10.47.61)

'Oh Shree Krishna, I will consider it my greatest good fortune to be born in my next life as a creeper, a bush, or a tree in Vrindavan. For then, I will receive the foot dust of the gopis (and become eligible to savour the divine bliss they are relishing).'

These are some of the reasons for worshipping the Lord in His Krishna form. However, as I had said earlier, choosing your *Iṣhṭa Dev* is a personal choice. You may worship any form of the Divine that appeals the most to you.

A clarification is necessary here. There are many celestial gods, such as Indra, Kuber, Vayu, Agni, and so on. They belong to the soul category and are not forms of the Supreme Divine Personality. Consider them to be like ministers in a government. There is a health minister, finance minister, agriculture minister, etc. After five years, when the government changes, all the ministers also change, and others occupy the same position.

Likewise, the celestial gods are not forms of the Supreme. They are souls who hold a celestial post for a certain period of time. When their tenure is over, they vacate their position, and another soul is appointed to it.

The Bhagavad Gita discourages us from worshipping celestial gods.

yānti deva-vratā devān pitṝīn yānti pitṛi-vratāḥ
bhūtāni yānti bhūtejyā yānti mad-yājino 'pi mām (9.25)

The verse explains that devotion to the celestial gods, the ancestors, and disembodied spirits will not lead to the supreme destination. Instead, we should attach our mind to the Supreme Divine Personality alone.

Do note that among the various Forms of the Almighty, we have a choice regarding the Form to worship—we can meditate on any Form of God that we desire. Understand this with an example. During the Diwali festival, sweets are made in many shapes—a man, a woman, a dog, a horse, a car, an elephant, etc. Children start fighting over them: 'I want the dog,' 'I want the horse,' and so on. The shopkeeper is amused and says, 'You can savour any of them, all are sweet.'

In conclusion, whether you worship God as Ram, Krishna, Shiv, or Narayan, They all are the same Supreme Entity.

CHANGING YOUR IṢHṬA DEV

Question: I have been worshipping Lord Ram since childhood. But now I am attracted to Shree Krishna. I am in a dilemma: if I switch my *Iṣhṭa Dev*, will it be considered an offence?

Answer: In the previous answer, it was explained that God is one. Ram, Krishna, Shiv, Ganesh, Narayan, Durga, and Parvati are various forms of the one Supreme Entity. Hence, as a personal preference, if you decide to change your *Iṣhṭa Dev,* there is nothing wrong with it.

If Ram and Krishna had been different personalities, there would have been scope for concern. But when They are the same Supreme all-powerful Lord, then why fear? In fact, many of the eternal associates of Shree Ram came again during the descension of Shree Krishna. They did not think their *Iṣhṭa Dev* had changed.

- Lakshman came as Balaram.
- Bharat came as Pradyumna (Shree Krishna's son).
- Shatrughna came as Aniruddha (Shree Krishna's grandson in Dwarika).
- Hanuman sat on the flag of Arjun's chariot to protect him during the Mahabharat war.
- Soorpanakha came as Kubja.
- Jambavant came in the same form and engaged in friendly combat with Shree Krishna.

The fear of changing *Iṣhṭa Dev* is, therefore, based on incorrect understanding. A wife sees her husband wearing casual attire at home in the evening. Next morning, he is in a formal suit while going to the office. She does not think her husband has changed. Similarly, a devotee of Shree Krishna, when he goes to the temple of Lord Ram, thinks, 'My Shree Krishna is in the form of a king here.'

Narsi Mehta is revered in history as a great poet-saint of Shree Krishna. He was initially a devotee of Lord Shiv. How he became a Krishna devotee is a fascinating story.

Narsi Mehta left home on one occasion and went to the temple of his Iṣhṭa Dev, *Lord Shiv. He prayed non-stop for seven days without partaking any food or water. Pleased with his devotion, Bhagavan Shiv appeared before him and offered to grant him a boon.*

The Saint bowed to Him and said, 'Give me whatever is dearest to You.'

The ever-compassionate Shivji gave Narsi Mehta a vision of Shree Krishna's Raas *leela with the gopis of Braj. When the Saint had the divine vision, he was enchanted by the beauty of Shree Krishna's three-fold-bending form. After granting this vision, Lord Shiv disappeared, and Narsi Mehta became a great devotee of Shree Krishna.*

In fact, take the case of Lord Shiv Himself. Although He is God, in His divine Pastimes, He worships Bhagavan Ram as His *Iṣhṭa Dev*. Yet, every time Shree Krishna descends, Lord Shiv goes to have His darshan. He even participated in the *Raas* leela of Shree Krishna, after taking on the form of a gopi.

In conclusion, the fear of sin in changing one's *Iṣhṭa Dev* exists only in our minds; it has no real basis.

POSITION OF RADHA

Question: Who was Radha, and why is She given so much importance in Shree Krishna bhakti?

Answer: Since eternity, God has taken on two forms—*Shakti* and *Shaktimān*—the Energy and the Energetic. Narayan and Lakshmi, Shiv and Parvati, Ram and Sita, and Krishna and Radha. Hence, Radha is not just a woman whom we see in temples sitting next to God; She is the divine Yogmaya power.

Yogmaya is the personal power of God with which He governs all His other powers. With the help of Yogmaya, God manifests His divine Abode and displays His divine Pastimes. Shree Krishna has also referred to it as *Atmamaya* in the Bhagavad Gita.

ajo 'pi sannavyayātmā bhūtānām īśhvaro 'pi san
prakṛitiṁ svām adhiṣhṭhāya sambhavāmyātma-māyayā

(verse 4.6)

'Although I am unborn, the Lord of all living entities, and have an imperishable nature, yet **I appear in this world by virtue of My *Atmamaya***, My divine power.'

This Yogmaya power takes on various Forms, such as Lakshmi, Durga, Kali, and Parvati. They are all worshipped as the Divine

Mother of the universe. They are all non-different from each other. Yet, there is a difference in the *rasa*.

Mother Durga is the form of Yogmaya where She is combating and subduing demons. She also oversees the material energy, maya. But Radha Rani is not concerned with any of this. She simply engages in the loving service of Shree Krishna and engages the souls in the same. She bestows the highest level of selfless divine love on the souls, and it is by Her grace that one attains Shree Krishna. Those who know this secret and wish to relish the sweetness of divine love worship the Divine Mother in Her sweetest form as Shree Radha.

In His inconceivable divine Pastimes, Krishna becomes subservient to Radha. The writings of Raskhan illustrate this.

dekhyau durau vah kuñj kutīr mein baiṭho paloṭat rādhikā pāyan

'Looking for Shree Krishna, when I finally got exhausted, He showed up in the kunj of Vrindavan, massaging Radha's lotus feet.'

This is, however, an esoteric subject. For our purpose, it is best to understand the unity between the *Shakti* and *Shaktimān*, between Radha and Krishna. The *Sāma Rahasyopaniṣhad* states:

anādirayaṁ puruṣhaṁ ekamevāsti tadeva rūpaṁ
dvidhāvidhāya samārādhana tatparobhūt tasmāt tāṁ
rādhāṁ rasikānandāṁ vedavido vadanti

'Since eternity, the one Supreme Lord has divided Himself in two Forms, the Energetic and the Energy. That Supreme

Energy (the Yogmaya power) is Radha, Who is worshipped by the knowers of the Vedas.'

14

Guru

HOW TO RECOGNIZE A GURU

Question: What is the way to find a true Guru? How can I evaluate if I have made the right choice and am moving on the correct path?

Answer: The choice regarding a Spiritual Master can impact your entire life's trajectory for better or for worse. Hence, it is a matter that requires careful thought and deliberation.

Who is a Guru? We use the word so often, but what does it really mean? 'Gu' means 'darkness' and 'ru' means 'to dispel'. Guru is the personality who dispels our darkness and ushers us into the light of divine knowledge. Even in material pursuits, an experienced and caring mentor makes a huge difference. The mentor on the spiritual path is known as the Guru.

The Guru is a divine personality. As per the Vedas, the Guru must possess two qualifications—*śhrotriya* and *brahma niṣhṭha*. The *Muṇḍaka Upanishad* states:

tadvijñānärtham sagurumeväbhigachchhet
samitpäniḥ shrotriyam brahmanishtham (1.2.12)

'To realize the Absolute Truth, approach with faith a Guru who is both *śhrotriya* and *brahma niṣhṭha*.' What do these terms mean?

***Śhrotriya* means 'knower of the scriptures'.** The Guru must possess the theoretical knowledge of the Vedic texts. Then he can explain erudite teachings based on the holy books, and it becomes easier for disciples to have faith in his teachings.

***Brahma niṣhṭha* means 'situated in God-realization'.** Only the one who has attained the Truth can help us do the same. This means that the Guru should be a practical plus theoretical person—one who has Vedic knowledge and has implemented these truths in his life.

The important question now is: how do we recognize a true guru? This is a difficult task. Compare it to a student in second grade of primary school assessing the relative competence of three college professors. Likewise, our intellect is material, so our assessment of the Guru is often inaccurate. Here are some blunders we commit.

First, we look for externals, such as His physical appearance, attire, and living accommodation. No wonder so many imposters wearing saffron robes manage to dupe innocent people in our society. Beware that it is not the colour of people's clothes that makes them holy but the colour of the heart, which should be steeped in devotion.

Second, in our quest for happiness, we seek material rewards based on incorrect beliefs. We look for gurus who offer worldly boons, such as wealth, health, and prestige. This only increases the business of charlatans and fake gurus. A true saint endows his followers with spiritual gifts—the wealth of divine love.

Third, we get tremendously impressed by supernatural acts, such as talking to spirits, levitating on water, and reading someone's mind. These are not spiritual powers; they are material siddhis (yogic powers). Faith that is based on the display of such siddhis is the crudest kind of devotional faith.

We must, instead, try to find a Saint endowed with spiritual siddhi. What kind of siddhi is this? The Guru possesses the ability to change the hearts of those who come in touch with him. A popular saying states:

pāras meṅ aru santoṅ meṅ, bahut antaro jān
vaha lohā kāñchan kare, vaha kare āpu samān

'A *paaras* (philosopher's stone) can only transform iron into gold but not into another *paaras.* But Saints can transform worldly people into Saints like themselves.'

Keeping the above safeguards in mind, let us learn how to recognize a spiritual teacher.

First, **when you associate with a true guru, you will naturally develop detachment from the world and attachment to God.**

Consider the example of a fire. If you are standing away from the fire on a wintery night, you feel cold. As you walk towards the fire, the cold vanishes, and you experience the heat.

Similarly, realized saints are like a ball of God-consciousness. When we come in contact with them, we naturally experience detachment from mundane worldly things and attachment to divine matters.

There is, however, a caveat here. The impact of a genuine saint varies from person to person, based on the purity of their own mind. It is much like the attraction between a magnet and needles.

Suppose you place five different needles, each with a different percentage of iron, around a magnet—one of pure iron; the second alloyed with a trace of copper; the third with a greater percentage of copper; the fourth with just a trace of iron; and the fifth of pure copper. What will happen?

A magnet attracts iron, so the pure iron needle will be instantly drawn to it. Other needles will be pulled less quickly, to the extent of the copper present. The needle with no iron will not experience any pull.

Similarly, on meeting a true saint, those with pure hearts will experience an immediate transformation, whereas those with impure hearts will be transformed slowly.

You may then ask, 'If am not experiencing any transformation in the association of a saint, what should I conclude? Is my heart so impure that I am not getting impacted? Or is the saint not a genuine one, and so there is no result?'

The solution is to do the satsang of many saints and then see where the impact is the most. Wherever the spiritual impact took place to the greatest extent, attach yourself to that personality. He is your Guru. If you use this formula in determining your Spiritual Master, you will not get cheated. That is because you are basing your decision on direct evidence—your own transformation.

Second, we find a true guru by the grace of God. When we have a sincere thirst for God, He leads us to our spiritual teacher. He also creates faith that helps us connect with our Guru. Jagadguru Kripaluji Maharaj has explained this cycle of spiritual quest beautifully:

hari kṛipā guru miley govind rādhey
guru kṛipā hari miley sab ko batā de (*Radha Govind Geet*)

'First, God will grace you and connect you with your Guru. Then the Guru will grace you and help you reach God.'

As the saying goes: 'God helps those who help themselves.' So, do not simply keep sitting for the Lord's grace to descend. Rather, search for a Guru yourself, and also pray to God for His blessings in the matter.

Once you reach the feet of a true saint, then stop running around from saint to saint. Instead, begin the process of practical sadhana under your Spiritual Master. Any further search is merely a distraction and a waste of time.

GURU MANTRA

Question: A lot of spiritual teachers emphasize taking a Guru mantra from them. What is your viewpoint on this?

Answer: Guru mantra is a ritual that has become popular in recent times. It is given in the ear of the disciple during diksha (initiation ceremony) by the Guru. People have come to believe that such diksha is the basis of the Guru-disciple relationship. Many are convinced that by simply receiving the Guru mantra, they will attain perfection.

However, this is an incomplete understanding. Getting the mantra does not constitute diksha, nor does it mean you will attain God. It also does not define the Guru-disciple relationship. Let us understand these concepts in detail.

The connection between the student and the teacher is much deeper than a paltry ritual. Real diksha is not merely the giving of a mantra in the ear of the disciple. Actual diksha means giving divine power to the disciple. It should result in liberation from maya and the attainment of divine knowledge, love, and bliss. It should initiate the disciple into the eternal Pastimes of God.

Such diksha is given by the Guru only when the disciple has fully cleansed his or her mind by doing 'Sadhan Bhakti'. Understand this through an example.

Let us say, you are building a house. You complete all the electrical fittings—the wiring, the fans, lights, switches, and meter boxes. But there is still no electricity in your home. You do not yet have a connection from the electrical station.

Now, the electrician from the electric company comes and joins the main wire of your house to the external power line. Instantly, there is light in your home.

Just as you first prepared your house and then set up the connection, similarly, you will first have to accept a Guru as your spiritual teacher. Then do sadhana under his guidance. This will purify your heart.

Once the vessel of the heart is prepared, you will then receive diksha, or the divine power from the Guru. This will result in God-realization and liberation from maya. This is real diksha, not merely the receiving of a mantra.

The problem arises because people do not care to purify their hearts. They look for shortcuts—so that they can retain all their worldly desires and also attain God. Claims of magic mantras, tantras, and yantras are very appealing to them. And gurus who offer such allurements become very popular.

We must remember that until the heart is totally cleansed, we will not achieve God-realization. And to cleanse the heart, we can chant any Name of God. There is no need for a special mantra.

Guru mantras are Sanskrit words such as *Śhrī kṛishṇa śharaṇaṁ mama, Om klīṅ kṛishṇāya namaḥ, Om rāṁ rāmāya namaḥ.* These mantras mean:

- *'O Shree Krishna, I surrender to You'*
- *'O Shree Krishna, I offer my obeisance to You'*
- *'O Lord Ram, I do namaste to You'*

They all express devotion to God. Whether you do so with the help of a mantra or in simple words, it is the sentiment that counts. In fact, if you do not utter even a single word, but keep a prayerful heart, the Lord will understand and reciprocate your sentiments. A beautiful story illustrates this.

A little girl would go to the temple daily, close her eyes with folded hands and mumble something for two minutes. She would then open her eyes, bow down, and run out. The temple priest would observe her with curiosity. He thought she was too young to know any prayers or mantras. One day, he asked, 'My child, I have been seeing you for many days now. What is it that you do every day?'

'I pray,' she said excitedly.

'But you are too small to know any prayers,' responded the priest. 'Then what do you mumble when you close your eyes?'

'I do not know any verses,' responded the girl, innocently. 'But I know A, B, C, D...up to Z. I recite it five times and tell God, "Please arrange the alphabet into the prayer that is most pleasing to you."'

The priest was overwhelmed at the little girl's simplicity of heart.

In the spiritual realm, inner feelings count, not our speech. God is the Knower of our hearts. There is no compulsion for complex mantras in sadhana; we can simply take the Name of God, which is the biggest mantra. The scriptures state:

samujhata sarisa nāma aru nāmī (*Ramcharitmanas*)

'There is no difference between God and His Name.' This means that the Name of God is the biggest mantra. Lord Shiv simply chants 'Ram Ram Ram...' Valmiki did not even do that. He chanted 'Ma...Ra...Ma...Ra,' and by doing so, he achieved the highest realization. Then what need is there of any other mantras apart from God's Name? Here a question arises.

Which Name of God should we chant? Some say it must be a particular name received in the ear from the Guru. However, Chaitanya Mahaprabhu refuted this.

nāmnāmakāri bahudhā nija-sarva-śhaktis

(*Śhikṣhāṣhṭakam* verse 2)

'Oh Shree Krishna! You have many Names. In each of these Names, You are sitting with all Your shaktis.'

Therefore, we can chant any of the innumerable Names of God. After all, Yashoda did not say, 'Shree Krishna' as we do. She used to say, 'Lala!' And her spiritual attainment was higher than even that of the greatest yogis.

God cares not for the words we utter. He is moved by the love in our hearts. And when we have love, we can chant any Name, such as Krishna, Govind, Damodar, Gopal, Ram, Shiv, or Narayan.

15

Fears and Struggles

FEAR OF THE UNKNOWN

Question: Swamiji, for no logical reason, I am often gripped by the fear of the unknown. It makes me wonder if this is because of my *prārabdh* karma. I do engage in sadhana, but I have not yet been able to get rid of fear. How can I overcome this affliction?

Answer: Fear is an instinctive response embedded in humans for self-protection. If it lasts a few moments, it is a helpful ally for self-protection in dangerous situations. But when fear gets blown out of proportion, it cripples our ability to function effectively. We realize its futility but feel helpless in averting it. So, let us see how we can get a handle on this obsessive emotion.

We all experience fear at some time or another. It could be the fear of a doctor's needle, a difficult year-end exam, a critical job interview, fear of insects, fear of heights, fear of the unknown, or any number of things. It could even be embedded deep in your subconscious because of a childhood experience. Perhaps a spider crawled over you, which left an everlasting mark on your mind. Now you get terrified every time a spider comes near you.

Whatever be its nature, if fear is inordinate, it sabotages rational thinking. That is why it is said that fear does not cripple death, it cripples life. But if we can overcome it, then victory lies on the other side. There is a famous Hindi song: *ḍar ke āge jīt hai* 'Beyond fear lies victory.' This is so true. Successful entrepreneurs were those who put aside the dread of uncertain results. The greatest Saints in history fearlessly ignored censure and walked the path of God.

To go beyond fear, let us understand what causes it.

The root cause of fear is attachment. This could be to bodily comfort, to a material situation, or to a person. Our mind clings to the subject of its attachment and fears separation from it. Sage Bhartrihari stated:

bhoge roge bhayaṁ kule chyutibhayaṁ vitte nṛpālād bhayaṁ
sarvaṁ vastu bhayāvahaṁ bhuvi nṛiṇāṁ vairāgyamevābhayaṁ
(*Vairagya Shatak* 31)

'If you are attached to sensual enjoyment, you will fear disease. If you are attached to a high position, you will dread downfall. If you are attached to wealth, you will dread penury. No matter what your mind clings to, you will experience fear. But the moment you become detached from material objects, you become unafraid.' This is the ultimate remedy for vanquishing fear.

Although detachment is the ultimate cure, it is not easy to accomplish. So, while you get there, here are some other techniques as well.

Explore the worst-case scenario of your fear. Invariably, you will realize that the reality is not as terrible as the mind is dreading it to be. So, make it a habit to question your fearful thoughts, 'What is the worst that could happen?'

Suppose you are attached to material comforts. Your constant debilitating fear is that they will get snatched away. Now, flip your perspective. Tell yourself, 'Okay, so what will happen if my fear comes true? Is the lack of a little bodily comfort really as awful as my mind has convinced me to believe?'

Make peace with the worst-case scenario, and the venomous fangs of fear will be removed.

Place your faith in God. He is our eternal Father and cares for us more than we care for ourselves. The *Pāṇḍav Gita* states:

> *bhojane chhādane chintāṁ vṛithā kurvanti vaiṣhṇavāḥ*
> *yo'sau viśhvambharo devaḥ sa bhaktān upekṣhate* (verse 76)

The verse says that devotees should not worry about food and clothing. God sustains the whole universe. Is He going to neglect His own devotees? Let us take inspiration from this story.

A young lady got married to a naval captain. She accompanied her husband on her first voyage across the ocean. Unfortunately, the ship got caught in a terrible storm. It was being tossed by waves on the high seas. This created tremendous fear among the passengers. The captain, however, remained completely calm.

Astonished on seeing his composure, the wife asked, 'My dear husband, when everyone is besieged by fear, how are you able to remain so calm?'

The captain unsheathed his sword and placed its naked blade on his wife's head. He said, 'Darling, are you feeling scared?'

'Why should I feel scared?' giggled the wife.

'But I have got the blade on your head,' the captain responded. 'It can go through your skull, killing you.'

'What a silly possibility to think of,' she said. 'The sword is in your hands, and you are my well-wisher. I have complete faith you will never harm me. Then why should I fear?'

'In the same way,' said the captain, 'I have complete faith that God is my well-wisher, and the ship is safe in His hands. He will always protect me. Whatever He does will be for my well-being.'

If we look around in the world, we see that the Lord takes care of all creatures. He provides for everyone from the tiny ants to giant elephants. Then what can be said of humans who place their trust in God?

Faith in God's protection does not mean, however, that He will fulfil our puny desires. It means that He is our benefactor. He will do whatever is good for our eternal spiritual emancipation.

DEALING WITH DISPARAGEMENT

Question: Swamiji, how should one deal with insults and denigration from others? While I am trying to join the bandwagon of positivity, I get totally derailed by such negativity. Please advise how I can learn to better handle such tense interactions.

Answer: Disparagement from others affects our confidence and makes us feel awful. Thus, most people seek to avoid it. Yet, there are some who know the art of not getting crushed when opposed. They take control of the situation without feeling helpless.

Effectively dealing with derisive behaviour requires emotional maturity. If we adopt constructive mindsets, we too will not be vulnerable. Here are three powerful techniques to help you handle others' condemnations.

You can never please everyone. There are varieties of natures in the world. Some people are naturally more loving and considerate, while others are disposed to being harsh and ruthless. The Bhagavad Gita identifies two kinds of persons:

dvau bhūta-sargau loke 'smin daiva āsura eva cha

(verse 16.6)

'People have two kinds of dispositions in the world—the divine and the demoniac.' Hence, no behaviour is universally appreciated. If you do good, the bad people will criticize you; if you do bad, the good people will condemn. Hence, seeking validation from everyone is futile. A popular folklore teaches us this moral.

A man took his grandson to town with their donkey. He made his grandson sit on the donkey while he walked alongside. A bystander saw them and was aghast. He remarked, 'Look at that selfish boy! He is sitting comfortably while the old man has to walk.' Feeling embarrassed, the grandfather took the boy off. Now, he rode the donkey with his grandson walking by the side.

A second passer-by came along and commented, 'What a selfish man! He is smugly sitting and making the little boy walk in this scorching heat.' Hearing this, the grandfather pulled up the little boy as well on to the donkey. Now, they both rode together.

Another passer-by came along and yelled, 'How cruel! You both are placing such a heavy load on the donkey!'

Now the grandfather had only one option left. He tied the donkey's four legs to a staff, and they both carried the creature on their shoulders. This time, everyone exclaimed, 'Both of them are totally crazy!'

The message is that no matter what you do, some will cleverly find fault. Even if you do your best, you cannot win. So, do not lose sleep over disapproval from others.

People have the right to their opinion; you have the right to disregard it. People will spill out what they hold inside. If they are full of frustration, they will pour it on to you. If they harbour goodness, they will shower you with it. Either way, do not take it personally. It is not about you but about them. Learn this profound lesson from the Buddha's story.

Once, a vile man approached the Buddha in a fit of fury and began cursing him. The Buddha listened calmly while the man continued his tirade with all his venom. After an hour, he got exhausted and stopped.

The Buddha said to his disciples, 'Give him some food and water, so he may regain his energy and begin again.'

The man was astonished, and said, 'Oh Sage! I said so many nasty things. But you did not even question why I was behaving badly. What is the secret of your peace?'

The Buddha responded, 'Suppose you give someone a gift and that person refuses to take it. With whom does the gift remain? Likewise, all that you offered me, I did not take it upon myself. It is still with you.'

When others criticize unduly, they are exercising their freedom. But you are not obliged to feel bad. You can refuse to take it by exercising your freedom. This is a simple way to insulate yourself from hurtful slander.

Look upon unfair vilification as purifying. We get disturbed by harsh words because we perceive them as harmful. But if spiritual progress is our goal, then negative people become an opportunity to purify our heart. By unjustifiably criticizing, they enable us to practise forbearance and cleanse our mind.

Saints exemplify such thinking. They are at ease with discomfort because it helps in developing tolerance and forgiveness. They use it to their advantage by growing in virtues.

Once an evil man considered a sage as his enemy, even though the sage had a mild and congenial nature. This person, however, was incorrigible; wherever he went, he would malign the holy man.

One day, the wicked man passed away. On hearing this, the sage's followers were relieved, in fact, overjoyed. They informed their Guru of his enemy's demise. But to their surprise, the sage became tearful. The disciples asked why he was so disturbed by the wretched man's death.

The Guru explained sagaciously, 'He was helping me in my sadhana. Because of him, I was learning tolerance and practising forgiveness. Now that he is no longer in my life, I am worried,

"How will I get purified?"'

We, too, should learn from this positive attitude towards vilifiers. Saint Kabir states:

niṅdak niyare rākhiye, āñgan kuṭi chhabāy
bin sābun pānī binā, nirmal kare subhāy

'If you are desirous of quickly cleansing your heart, cultivate the company of a critic. Your heart will be cleansed without water and soap when you tolerate their acrimonious words.'

When we make spiritual growth our prime motive, we too will welcome adversarial circumstances as God-sent opportunities for progress. Then, we will remain equanimous in both praise and denunciation.

FORGIVENESS

Question: How can we forgive those who have wronged us? And how can we be sure that we have truly forgiven, with no trace of a grudge remaining within?

Answer: Learning to forgive is very important for everyone because we have all been wronged in life. Maybe people deceived us and broke our trust. Possibly, our loved ones turned their backs on us. Or we may even have suffered abuse at their hands. These hurts can be traumatic, filling our heart with resentment. The practice of forgiveness is the recourse to healing wounds.

What is forgiveness? It is the conscious decision to release bitterness towards our wrongdoers. We deliberately choose to pardon, while eschewing the urge to retaliate. Doing so heals emotional pain that would otherwise fester in our mind. Thus, we feel at peace and can move on with our life.

Lack of forgiveness comes with a slew of side effects. It makes us anxious or even depressed. It brings anger into our relationships and changes the way we connect with others. Resentment comes at a heavy price. **This is why forgiveness is a gift we bestow on ourselves.**

Let us learn how to cultivate this sublime virtue.

Understand that people are imperfect. If they behave selfishly, what is so surprising? They are under maya, with the material imperfections of anger, greed, desire, and pride. It is only natural that they will make mistakes. When we are empathetic, we will be more forgiving towards their misbehaviour.

Use hurts to your advantage. Look for the silver lining in the clouds—how you can benefit from the incident. For example, if your business partner betrays you, use the experience to realize, 'I must not put my trust in worldly people. I must reserve unquestioning faith for God and Guru alone'.

If your friend cheats you, become cognizant, 'I have no true friend in the world except God.' In this way, derive spiritual benefit from the ill behaviour of others.

Realize that forgiving is necessary to move on in life. Harbouring ill feelings towards anyone sullies our mind. It gets stuck in repetitive resentful thoughts. We are then ensnared in bitterness and cannot progress spiritually. This is why Jagadguru Kripaluji Maharaj says:

bhūlihuñ durbhāvanā kahuñ, ho na sapanehuñ pyāre
(Sādhanā Karu Pyāre)

'Even in your dreams, do not make the mistake of harbouring ill will towards anyone.'

What is the sign of true forgiveness? When we no longer feel resentful on remembering our hurt, we have truly forgiven. It does not mean we have forgotten the wrongdoings, but the memories no longer evoke negative emotions. You have moved on by accepting the situation and relieving yourself of its burden.

Let me conclude the answer with a beautiful story on the power of forgiveness.

Amy Biehl was a Stanford graduate. She had won the Fulbright Scholarship to assist the anti-apartheid movement, in particular, women's rights in South Africa. One day, when Amy was driving by, a riot broke out and she was dragged out of her car and killed by a mob of blacks. In their fury towards whites, they were unaware she had left her luxurious American life to join their struggle for equal rights.

Amy's parents, Linda and Peter, were plunged into an ocean of grief when they heard the news. After years of hurt and bitterness, they chose to forgive. They left California and moved to South Africa to continue their daughter's work. They got acquainted with two of Amy's killers. From them, they learnt of the tumultuous circumstances of the riot and were touched by the heartfelt remorse of the murderers.

The young men who had killed Amy atoned by providing voluntary service to the Biehl Foundation established in her name. With time, they became close to the Biehls, and even addressed Linda Biehl as 'Mom'. Today, these men are community leaders, working for the welfare of those affected by the apartheid.

What an amazing unheard-of story! Hats off to the Biehls for not only forgiving their daughter's killers but also transforming them into social leaders. Forgiveness uplifts both the forgiver and the forgiven because of its inherent selfless nature. It is a sublime personality trait to inculcate in ourselves and a sure sign of spiritual maturity.

16

Wisdom for Everyday Living

PRACTISING AUSTERITIES

Question: Lord Krishna emphasizes the importance of austerities in the Bhagavad Gita. What kind of austerities should we follow in modern living?

Answer: Austerities in the modern world are not as intimidating as the word sounds. These are not the gruelling rigours performed by sages in ancient times. They are timeless practices we can follow to gain control over our own mind and senses. This, in turn, helps to elevate our life and enables our authentic, higher self to shine. Let us look at what austerities mean to us.

Tapasya, or austerity, is the voluntary acceptance of discomfort for the accomplishment of a higher purpose. It cleanses the body, mind, and intellect by restraining them from seeking and enjoying material pleasures. In addition, it also develops the ability to endure hardships for worthwhile goals in life. Consequently, we let go of limiting beliefs and self-doubts.

Hence, austerity is extremely purifying. The essence is to curtail the natural propensity of the senses and mind to seek pleasure in material objects. These austerities are of three kinds—of the body, speech, and mind. Shree Krishna has elaborated on each of these in the Bhagavad Gita in verses 17.14–16.

Austerities of the body. The human body experiences worldly pleasures through its five senses—sight, smell, touch, taste, and hearing. The creator, Brahma, has made these senses outwardly facing. If left uncontrolled, the senses become our biggest enemy. If given an inch, they demand a mile. They are the ones that trap us in gluttony, indulgence, and addictions.

Therefore, austerity of the body is to hold the senses in check—restraining them from their objects of enjoyment. This includes abstaining from all sensual enjoyment, in general, and sexual indulgence, in particular.

Austerities of speech. This involves controlling our tongue, and uttering only words that are beneficial, truthful, inoffensive, and pleasing to the listener. Speech austerities also include chanting Vedic hymns, Names of God, and bhajans and kirtans. The progenitor, Manu, wrote:

satyaṁ brūyāt priyaṁ brūyān na brūyāt satyam apriyam
priyaṁ cha nānṛitaṁ brūyād eṣha dharmaḥ sanātanaḥ

(*Manu Smṛiti* 4.138)

'Speak the truth in such a way that it is pleasing to others. Do not speak the truth in a manner injurious to others. Never speak untruth, though it may be pleasant. This is the eternal path of morality and dharma.'

Austerities of the mind. These involve keeping the mind clear of negative and impure thoughts. Instead, fill your consciousness with sublime and noble ideas. Make your emotions serene and gentle. Practise mental silence, free from the chatter of unnecessary thoughts. Let every thought be deliberate and well-intended. All of these are declared as the austerities of the mind.

We must sincerely tend to the garden of our mind, seeding it with good and gracious thoughts. Also, we must be ever-alert in weeding out negative thoughts that have a debilitating effect on our psyche. These are the poisons that choke out divine grace from manifesting in our heart.

By sincerely practising these austerities, we can purify our life and consciousness. A word of caution here. Although austerity is a powerful tool for cleansing, not everyone utilizes it with pure motives.

The intention behind austerities is what counts. For example, a politician works tirelessly to give multiple speeches a day. This is also a form of austerity. But since it is done for position and power, it does not purify. Similarly, if one engages in religious austerities with the idea of achieving honour and prosperity, the intent is material.

Austerity becomes perfect when it pleases God. He is: *bhoktāraṁ yajña-tapasāṁ* 'The Supreme Enjoyer of all sacrifices and austerities.'

Therefore, **the highest austerity is to engage the body, mind, and intellect in the service of God.** In this divine consciousness, one uses the eyes to see the Form of God everywhere in the world, and the tongue to chant His glories. The mind is engaged in loving remembrance of God and Guru. And every action is done as an offering to the Supreme.

VEGETARIAN DIET

Question: Why does Hinduism recommend a vegetarian diet?

Answer: Our diet impacts our entire personality. After digestion, the grossest portion of food is excreted, the subtler portion goes to make our body, while the subtlest portion makes the mind.

There is a Hindi saying: *jaisā aṅn vaisā mana*. It means that the kind of food you eat influences the nature of your mind as well. In verses 17.8–17.10, the Bhagavad Gita describes three types of food and their impact on our consciousness and body.

Sattvic foods. These include grains, pulses, beans, fruits, vegetables, milk, and other vegetarian foods. They are juicy, succulent, nutritious, and naturally tasteful. They promote superior health, joyfulness, and contentment.

Rajasic foods. These include foods containing excessive chillies, sugar, and salt. When sattvic foods are too sweet, too salty, too sour, too hot, or too cold, they become rajasic. The goal now is no longer nutrition but titillation of the palate. Such diets in the mode of passion adversely impact health. They affect the mind by igniting insatiable material ambitions, resulting in restlessness and distress.

Tamasic foods. These comprise overcooked, stale, polluted, and impure foods. In the mode of ignorance are also included meat, fish, and eggs. They result in clouding of the intellect and increased anger, laziness, intoxication, and violence.

From the above analysis, it is clear that a simple vegetarian diet is conducive to nurturing virtues in the mode of goodness, which are so helpful for spiritual progress. Vegetarian food also promotes longevity (*āyuḥ sattva*) and good health.

The *Chhāndogya Upanishad* echoes the same sentiment: *āhāra śhuddhau sattva śhuddhiḥ* (7.26.2) 'By eating pure food, the mind becomes pure.'

The human body was not designed for consuming meat. Let us learn about indicators that nature intended humans to be vegetarian.

- Carnivorous animals have a full set of canine teeth that can tear through flesh. Humans, on the other hand, have only four canines, while they possess 12 molars for grinding vegetables and grains.
- Carnivorous creatures also have higher acidity levels in their stomach for processing flesh. Vegetarians and humans have lower stomach acidity, geared to digesting pre-chewed vegetarian foods.
- Again, carnivores have shorter intestines because meat putrefies fast. It needs to be expelled rapidly from the body. Human intestines, on the other hand, are about six times the body length. If meat stays in the body for that long, it begins to decay. That is why medical science states that

meat eaters are at a significantly higher risk of cancer than non-meat eaters.[4]

Some famous personalities who practised vegetarianism were Benjamin Franklin, Pythagoras, William Shakespeare, Leonardo da Vinci, Leo Tolstoy, and Mahatma Gandhi. George Bernard Shaw, who was also a vegetarian, stated the reason for his choice: 'I do not want to make my stomach a graveyard of dead animals.'

In conclusion, even though the scriptures do not forbid us from eating meat, they make us aware of the consequences. They clearly promote the benefits of a sattvic diet. There is now a growing awareness that a vegetarian diet will not only save us but also the planet.

BALANCING DUTIES TO GOD AND FAMILY

Question: How should I handle conflicts in my duties towards God and the world? What is the best way to balance time between spirituality, work, and family?

Answer: 'What is my duty?' is a question that continues to intrigue humankind from time immemorial. Arjun asked this question to Shree Krishna more than 5,000 years ago. And even today, if you do a quick search on Google, you will find over a

[4]'New Study Finds Lower Risks of Cancer for Vegetarians, Pescatarians and Low Meat-Eaters', *Oxford Population Health*, 24 February 2022, https://tinyurl.com/4xym5k3w. Accessed on 9 August 2023.

billion results for this query.

People have multiple responsibilities in life—they have duties towards family, company, society, and country. Yet, some remain unsatisfied even after executing these duties. Their search for fulfilment and inquiry steers them to spirituality.

From the scriptures and the Guru, understand that our true identity is the 'soul'. And **the eternal relative of the soul is God, towards whom we have spiritual duties.** He sits in our heart and stays with us in every lifetime. Hence, He is our eternal Father, Mother, Friend, and Well-wisher. Doing our spiritual duties towards Him is 'bhakti'.

Performing our social duties well ensures the well-being of people around us and creates harmony in society. It lifts us from tamas and rajas to sattva (the mode of goodness).

Performing our spiritual duties well ensures the ultimate purification of our mind. It lifts us to the nirguna state (beyond the three gunas). We attract divine grace and finally achieve God-realization.

There is a small section of people who forsake all other duties and perform their duties towards God alone. These are karm sanyasis (renunciant monks). They are a very minuscule section of society. For the vast majority, karm yog is recommended. **Karm yogis are those who perform both spiritual and material duties.**

Now, as a karm yogi, the problem invariably arises when we devote more time than necessary to our material duties. In the process, our spiritual duties get neglected. To avoid this slip-up, we must always remember our foremost duty is to make our life a success by attaching our mind to God. So, let us not forget to allot a certain amount of time every day for devotion. A simple rule of thumb here is to dedicate one to two hours daily for spiritual sadhana, as explained in the question 'How Should I Set Up My Daily Practice?'. With that taken care of, everything else will nicely fall into place.

Take stock of all your material activities. Is there anything you can eliminate? The art of saying 'No' to whatever does not add value is a powerful mantra. Steve Jobs, the founder of Apple, took immense pride in his ability to say 'No'. He said, 'I'm actually as proud of the things we haven't done as the things I have done.'

Tim Cook, the current CEO of Apple, continues the same legacy, 'We believe in saying no to thousands of projects so that we can really focus on the few that are truly important and meaningful to us.'

So, evaluate all your commitments. You will realize that many are not necessary but are taking up valuable time. It is safe to discard them.

Now that you have narrowed down your list of duties, allocate time to each. For example, you could allocate eight hours to your job, an hour for daily sadhana, an hour with your kids, and an hour for your exercise. Make a schedule and stick to it.

When you are at work for eight hours, give it your best. While at work, stay focussed, but then, on leaving the office, switch off from work. When spending time with your children, give them your full attention. Children do not need you to devote 24 hours to playing with them. But they do require your undivided attention during the little time you do spend with them.

People make the mistake of staying distracted and checking their phones. Focus, instead, on one task at a time and give it your best. Similarly, when it is time for your sadhana, avoid distractions and concentrate completely on attaching your mind to God.

Further, **remember the difference between performing your duties and getting attached** to family and profession. Introspect and ask, 'Am I doing my duty towards my children or am I overly attached to them?'

For example, in your parental duties, you help your child prepare for an exam. Suppose the child does not do well. Now, if you are attached to your child, you will experience immense sadness. But if you are doing it as your duty, the result will not disturb you. You will think, 'It's all right, I did my duty as a parent. We will try harder next time.'

In this way, **become a karm yogi, and do your duties without attachments.** This verse from the Bhagavatam nicely describes the balance between spiritual and worldly duties:

gṛiheṣhv āviśhatāṁ chāpi puṁsāṁ kuśhala-karmaṇām
mad-vārtā-yāta-yāmānāṁ na bandhāya gṛihā matāḥ

(Shreemad Bhagavatam 4.30.19)

'The perfect karm yogis, even while fulfilling their household duties, perform all their works as yajna to Me, knowing Me to be the Enjoyer of all activities. They spend whatever free time they have hearing and chanting My glories. Such people, though living in the world, never get bound by their actions.'

As you progress spiritually and learn to offer all your actions to God, the conflict between the spiritual and material spheres will begin to diminish. Eventually, the stage will arrive when everything you do will become an offering to God. Then, there will be no dire need to balance your time. That is what Saint Kabir said:

jahañ jahañ chalūñ karūñ parikramā, jo jo karūñ so sevā
jab sovūñ karūñ daṇḍvat jānūñ dev na dūjā

'Whenever I walk, I think I am circumambulating the Lord; when I work, I see it as seva. While sleeping, I cultivate the sentiment of offering obeisance to the Supreme. In this way, my every work is devotion and service.'

PRIDE AT WORK

Question: Some level of pride is necessary for influencing others in the corporate environment. But you tell us not to harbour pride. Then how will people take us seriously?

Answer: It is a misconception that we need to harbour pride to be successful at work. Our ability to influence others does not come from a sense of self-importance. Rather, it is a result of virtuous personality traits, such as humility, combined with expertise in our field.

If we stay devoid of pride, we can be our authentic self. We do not need to put on a farce. This puts our mind at ease and helps us focus on our work.

Without pride, our mind is open to learning from others. We do not feel threatened by others' perspectives and viewpoints. Rather, we accord them due respect, engendering inclusivity at work. When we keep aside our ego, we are less vulnerable to being hurt. We can readily own our imperfections and weaknesses. This makes us more 'human' and easy to connect with at a deeper level. We easily accept and apologize for our mistakes. This wins the trust and respect of others.

For all the above reasons, humility is a personality strength and not a weakness as many would believe. Conceit, in contrast, morphs into feelings of superiority. It makes us play 'king of the hill'. Others are discouraged from collaborating with us because they feel intimidated. We end up losing their respect and trust.

On a team level, egotism can shift focus from team spirit to spotlighting our own accomplishments. This can demoralize others. Hence, pride is unattractive and counterproductive. It compromises our work and relationships, which is a far cry from creating a positive impact at work.

The finest leaders and CEOs are most humble yet highly successful. They are high performers and bring out the best in others. Take inspiration from Ratan Tata, former chairman of Tata Sons.

Ratan Tata had the ambition of launching a car designed entirely in India. His efforts bore fruit with the launch of Tata Indica in 1998. It was also the world's cheapest car. However, Indica fared poorly in the market, and Tata Motors decided to sell the division. Ford Motor Company expressed interest in buying it. So, Ratan Tata flew to Detroit with his team. To his surprise, he was humiliated by the chairman, Bill Ford, who said, 'You know nothing about cars; why did you get into it? We are doing you a favour by buying the division.'

That evening, after the meeting, Ratan Tata was pensive. He quietly flew back to India with his team, without selling the car business. He now turned his attention to the automobile industry. By 2008, Tata Motors had gained a significant presence in the worldwide market. Interestingly, the wheel of fate had turned around, and Ford Motor Company was now struggling.

Tatas offered to buy out their worst-selling brands—Jaguar and Land Rover. This time, Bill Ford flew over to Mumbai with his team. Humbled, he now expressed, 'You are doing us a favour by purchasing these two product lines.'

Ratan Tata had the opportunity to humiliate Ford in return for the insult he had received years ago. But he remained gracious and respectful. Today, he is one of the most respected business leaders in the world.

Thus, never harbour the misconception that to be effective at work, you need to be conceited. On the contrary, success follows those who are humble. In every environment, freedom from vanity is an adorning asset of one's personality. Finally, it also attracts divine grace for God hates pride and loves humility.

DEALING WITH DEPRESSION

Question: Swamiji, how can we deal with depression? Is there a spiritual solution to this material problem?

Answer: Depression has become a commonplace modern-day affliction. The World Health Organization (WHO) estimates that globally, 280 million people or more than 5 per cent of the adult population suffers from depression.[5] It is a mental health condition that impacts daily life, functionality, and relationships.

What does depression look like? It is marked by feelings of melancholy and hopelessness for an extended period of time—typically two weeks or more. Additional symptoms include change in appetite, fatigue, difficulty sleeping, loss of interest in everyday activities, feeling worthless, physical pain, and trouble concentrating. At its worst, one can experience suicidal thoughts.

Depression is a very complex disease to understand. It is not simply brought on by an imbalance of brain chemicals. There are numerous potential causes, such as poor mood regulation by the brain, genetics, medical conditions, and traumatic life events, among others.

Since the onset of depression has a variety of reasons, holistic treatment is ideal. It can include proper diet, exercise, yoga, counselling, medication, cognitive therapy, and spiritual wisdom. In this book, we focus on the spiritual aspect as an antidote to depression.

Physiological reasons apart, **depression arises when one feels:**

---

[5]'Depressive Disorder (Depression)', *World Health Organization*, 31 March 2023, https://tinyurl.com/mvhhktwc. Accessed on 9 August 2023.

1) I have failed in life, 2) there is no hope for success, 3) I can never be happy. Examples of pessimistic thoughts are: 'The whole world is against me', 'No one understands me', 'I can never succeed', 'Everyone else is doing better than I am', 'Life will never be the same again', and so on. Such negative thinking, when it continues long-term, plunges people into depressive states.

Unfortunately, these emotions have become commonplace nowadays because of rampant materialism. People firmly believe that happiness lies in material prosperity—fame, riches, beauty, and status. Social media gives the impression that others who possess these are happier than us. So, we chase them. And when our expectations are not fulfilled, we fall into despair. That negative thought pattern, when repeated, results in depression.

Thus, to overcome depression, we must purge negative thoughts and toxicity from our mind. Spiritual wisdom trains us to keep our mind elevated at all times. Here are two powerful spiritual mindsets to cultivate to retain your peace amidst challenges.

The attitude of gratitude is a big antidote for toxic emotions and poisonous thought patterns. We must train ourselves to be thankful to God for the gifts we have received and stop taking them for granted. These include the food we eat, the air we breathe, the earth we walk upon, and much more.

During the Covid-19 pandemic, a billionaire became critically ill. He was taken to the ICU of a premium hospital and put on the ventilator. After a week, the ventilator came off, and he was ready to go back home. The hospital handed him a bill of 10 lakh rupees.

Seeing it, he began crying. This surprised the front desk officer, and he asked, 'Sir, we all know you are worth billions. Why are you so disturbed about this 10 lakh rupees charge?'

'I am not crying because I cannot pay it,' said the billionaire. 'I am thinking, "God has been supplying me with oxygen since I was born, and He never sent me a bill." I am shedding tears in gratitude to Him.'

This man finally realized the magnitude of God's grace upon him. Most of us are like him in this matter. We keep whining about our deficiencies, while conveniently forgetting our blessings. Instead, we can become far happier by learning to cultivate a thankful heart.

Martin Seligman, who is considered the father of positive psychology, tried this experiment on 50 depression patients. He asked them to write three things daily they were grateful for. Within two months, 94 per cent had come out of depression and that too without drugs.[6]

Have faith that God is our well-wisher. In the face of difficulties—when challenges seem colossal—we can feel hopeless. Instead of being despondent in such times, we must take solace in God's protection and compassion for us. The Shreemad Bhagavatam states:

pīta-prāye 'mṛite devair bhagavān loka-bhāvanaḥ (8.9.27)

'Bhagavan is the best Friend and Well-wisher of the three worlds.' He is our eternal Father and the benevolent Caretaker

---

[6]Seligman, Martin E.P., 'Positive Psychology: A Personal History', *Annual Review of Clinical Psychology*, Vol. 15, No. 1–23, May 2019, https://tinyurl.com/3hhk7cpu. Accessed on 9 August 2023.

of all living beings. We must have faith that God is looking out for us. Take inspiration from the following story.

A businessman was sitting next to a little girl on a flight. Seeing that she was travelling alone, he engaged in small talk with her.

An hour into the flight, the plane started to experience severe turbulence. Everyone was told to put on their seatbelts and remain calm. The plane took drastic dips, shaking tumultuously. The passengers started sweating, praying, and clutching their seats.

Meanwhile, the little girl was unmoved and sat quietly next to the terrified businessman. She neatly put away her colouring book and crayons and sat with her hands calmly resting on her legs. The turbulence soon ended. The businessman was astonished at the girl's bravery and asked, 'Dear, how did you remain so calm while all of us adults were horrified?'

Looking him in the eye, the girl remarked, 'My father is the pilot, and he is taking me home. I am not worried.'

The girl's sense of secureness came from her awareness that her father was the pilot of the plane. Likewise, make God the Driver of your life. He is the Master of infinite universes and our loving Guardian. If we put our complete faith in Him, He will do everything to protect us no matter how pitiable our situation may be. And even the biggest reversal is part of His great plan for us. Such absolute faith in God lifts us from despondency.

HOW TO DEAL WITH BULLIES

Question: Sometimes we become the target of bullies. Should we ignore them or retaliate? What is the right way to deal with them, while retaining our calm?

Answer: As spiritual seekers, we naturally cherish and practise the virtues of gentleness and forgiveness. But the people we interact with are of all kinds. So, we should not be surprised when others insult us, behave badly with us, or bully us. Their bad behaviour is not about us but about them. They are simply acting out of their lower nature.

Imagine a bull gone crazy. Its very nature is to hit people and things. It will not discriminate between those who are vegetarians and those who are not; it will simply act by its disposition. Likewise, people will behave with you as per their own nature. Therefore, it is naïve to expect, 'I am a good person, so everyone should behave well with me.'

Our immediate reaction to insults should not be anger. This is the weakest and easiest response. It conveys lack of control over our emotions. In fact, it damages our position by empowering the person insulting us. They now know our sensitivity to their words and actions. So, whenever they wish to make us furious, they will press the same button again.

This does not mean, however, that we should meekly allow others to exploit us. The Vedic scriptures advise us to take necessary action for protecting ourselves when attacked.

In the next step, **we should firmly convey that we do not accept their unpleasant behaviour.** There will be consequences if it does not stop. Consequences do not mean that you argue with them. It may simply mean not speaking with them, not being available for them, not responding to their messages, or even firmly letting them know your mind. Any of these will ensure that the bullies know you are not a pushover. Quite likely, they will move out of your life.

The intention is not to punish but to establish a respectful boundary. Hence, it should be done with sympathy in the heart and not with a feeling of payback. So, choose a response that discourages the bully, without poisoning your own mind. Learn from this charming story.

In a neighbourhood, there lived a venomous and foul-tempered snake. The children of that locality feared it greatly. The moment they spotted it at a distance, they would run for their life.

One day, Sage Naṛad happened to come to that area. As was the snake's habit, it approached the sage with its hood raised menacingly and eyes fiercely red. Naradji, however, stood his ground peacefully, wearing a benevolent smile on his face.

The snake was astonished, and asked, 'Everyone runs from me in fear. How come you are not scared of me? Oh great sage, teach me the secret of your serenity.'

Naradji taught the snake the process of devotion, whereupon the snake became his disciple and began practising bhakti. It then shunned violence. Soon the children came to know that the snake was harmless and would not bite anyone. Now their fear vanished. On sighting it, they would bombard it with a battery of sticks and stones. They would even come close and kick it with their heeled shoes. The poor snake was badly injured.

One year later, Naradji was visiting that area again. He thought, 'Let me see how my disciple is doing.' He was dismayed to see the snake in a terrible state, with wounds all over his body. 'What happened to you, my dear disciple?' he inquired.

'Oh Gurudev, this is the result of the bhakti that you taught me,' replied the snake. 'The people of the world—knowing I will not retaliate—do not let me live peacefully.'

Naradji then explained, 'I asked you to stop biting people, but I did not say you should stop spreading your hood. Whenever the children attack, simply raise your head and hiss loudly. Then no one will come near you.'

Thenceforth, whenever the children came close, the snake would begin hissing and frighten them all away. Soon, it was living peacefully again.

Similarly, on the path of devotion, we should shun actions and thoughts directed at harming others, but we have the right to perform legitimate actions to prevent being perceived as a soft target.

17

Service and Giving

SADHANA VS SEVA

Question: In spirituality and in bhakti, which is more important: sadhana or seva?

Answer: This is like asking which is healthier—drinking water or eating food. The correct answer is both are essential. Similarly, both seva and sadhana are necessary for a sadhak.

Sadhana deepens our loving relationship with God. It also helps us work on our defects and grow our virtues. During sadhana, we plead God to bestow the opportunity to serve Him. We develop the aspiration to give all we have, without seeking anything in return. That's when the seed of selfless love is sown within us. However, only when we step into the arena of seva does sadhana sprout into something profound.

By doing seva, we put our learning into practice. It helps us realize that devotion is to be done for the happiness of God. Through service, we grow in selflessness, which is essential for divine love. Seva also prepares us for the divine seva of God in His nitya leela (eternal Pastimes) in His Abode.

Seva is, thus, the very life of bhakti. In fact, the original nature of the soul is to serve God. The *Chaitanya Charitāmṛit* states:

jīvera svarūpa haya kṛiṣhṇera nitya-dāsa

(*Madhya Leela* 20.108)

'The soul is by nature the servant of God.' Hence, seva is the supreme goal that we must strive for.

Now understand the entire link:

- Serving God in His nitya leela, or eternal Pastimes, is the ultimate goal of the soul.
- For such divine service, we need 'Siddha Bhakti' (divine love for God).
- 'Siddha Bhakti' will be bestowed upon us when our heart is eligible for receiving it.
- To purify our heart, we must engage in 'Sadhan Bhakti' (preparatory devotion). Therefore, 'Sadhan Bhakti' is the first step.

While practising 'Sadhan Bhakti', we must pay attention to both aspects—seva and sadhana.

When you engage in seva, you interact with people and things. This wears out your mind and tends to make it worldly. You have to counter it with sadhana, which cleanses the mind and re-establishes it in divine consciousness. In this way, seva and sadhana go hand in hand.

Eventually, the distinction between sadhana and seva disappears. This happens when the sadhak's only thought is to please God and Guru. At that stage, even sadhana is done for Their happiness. And then, the sadhak reaches a stage where both sadhana and seva become one and the same.

HOW TO SERVE

Question: What are the ways in which I can serve God?

Answer: There are four kinds of seva described in our scriptures: those done with dhan (wealth), tana (body), mana (mind), and atma samarpan (offering our soul).

Serving the Lord through our wealth is the first step. Whatever you earn, give a portion of it for the pleasure of God. This simple act of sacrifice changes our attitude towards our profession. While earlier our goal was to earn wealth for worldly enjoyment, dhan seva transforms this perspective. We develop the thought, 'I am earning money so that I may serve God and Guru with it.'

Such thinking one day culminates in karm yog. Then, even while working, the mind remains attached to God. But to reach this elevated stage, offering a portion of our earnings in seva is the first step.

Higher than dhan seva is serving with the body. In tana seva, you do physical seva, such as volunteering for temple activities. This can be done through any of the numerous spiritual organizations in the world.

If JKYog is your organization of choice, you can volunteer at the local satsang centres, retreats, temples, or for online activities. You can contribute your expertise to JKYog's multifarious projects. Or help spread the word about our programmes so more souls can benefit. We have a large global network of volunteers from different walks of life. They devote their time and energy to serving God and Guru. You can read more about it at: *www.jkyog.org/volunteer* and *www.jkyog.in/volunteer.*

Even higher than tana seva is mana seva. This means serving with our mind. It entails constantly harbouring the thought, 'I seek to give happiness to God and Guru'. When we serve with our mind, we naturally engage the body and wealth in service as well. So, mana seva automatically results in tana seva and dhan seva.

The highest seva is atma samarpan, which means to offer our soul itself in the service of the Lord. When we surrender our 'self', we have nothing further to give. The soul, however, is coupled to the mind. So, atma samarpan can only happen when our mind is completely and exclusively absorbed in God.

Therefore, to reach atma samarpan, we must begin with the first step—dhan seva. Start by offering a portion of your earnings to the Lord. In this matter, the principle of miserly people is *chamaḍī jāye par damaḍī na jāye* 'I can let go of my skin (life), but not my wealth.' Consequently, their mind remains attached to worldly things.

Instead, if we offer a percentage of our earnings in service, we slowly get inspired to serve with our body as well. And when we begin doing tana seva, we physically enter the devotional environment. Then the mind becomes immersed in thoughts of the Divine, and we progress to manasi seva.

Finally, we reach the stage of *sarveṣhu kāleṣhu mām anusmara* or constant remembrance of the Supreme. Then, all our activities automatically get dedicated to God. For example, the thoughts become 'I must eat to nourish my body, so I can serve God and Guru with it', 'I am reading so I can gain knowledge and serve Him better', and so on.

In this way, when the mind stays absorbed in thoughts of seva, then atma samarpan naturally takes place.

18

About Swamiji

SWITCHING FROM IIT AND IIM TO SANYAS

Question: You are an alumnus of two distinguished institutions —IIT Delhi and IIM Calcutta. It is intriguing to see you renounced a promising career and took sanyas. What made you change your stance in life and become a spiritual leader? Was it prompted by a specific event in life or was it a process?

Answer: Many believe that people turn to spirituality for solace when life falls apart. They think maybe disappointment in love or downfall in career is the only reason impelling people to don saffron robes. However, this stereotype is a misunderstanding that must be dismantled.

In my personal experience, turning to spirituality was not because of some dramatic episode, but a very natural process. When I look back, it seems God had designed my life for the spiritual path. Even earning the IIT and IIM stamps in my profile was arranged by Him. Although as a child, I grew up all over the country, when I reached grade eight, my father was transferred to Delhi as part of his job. This provided an opportunity for good education, which resulted in my entry into IIT.

As an eighth grader, I came across a book on energizing the powers of the mind. Inspired by it, I began practising meditation and yog nidra. These were non-devotional meditational practices, but I continued them throughout my student life.

Now, coming to the main point—how the spiritual spark got ignited. At IIT, the education included equations, models, and theories. I noticed that technological formulae would start with an assumption. Then, in the sequence of logical deductions, further assumptions would be made.

Science taught the laws of nature, but there was no mention of the Lawmaker. While common sense suggested that if there are laws, there should be a Lawmaker as well. This convinced me that present-day scientific knowledge could not help me know the Absolute Truth.

Then, at IIM, studies included a whole array of humanities subjects, including economics, psychology, sociology, and organizational behaviour. In each, many conflicting theories existed. For example, in psychology, Freud, Jung, Adler, Skinner, Maslow, and Rogers—all had differing opinions about the human psyche. This led me to conclude that they were all guessing, and none of them knew the Absolute Truth.

The academic scenario also left the bigger questions of life unanswered. I yearned to know, 'Who am I?', 'What is the purpose of life?', 'Why did I come into this world?', and 'Who is my Creator?' This is when I began delving into the scriptures—

Bhagavad Gita and Shreemad Bhagavatam. On reading these holy books, suddenly the whole puzzle fell into place. Both head and heart exclaimed, 'Yes, this is it!' Then I started engaging in bhakti, and as a result, my mind got attached to God.

After graduating from IIM, I joined the corporate world and was working at Tata Burroughs, India's first IT company. However, learning the Burroughs mainframe computer and its financial package did not satisfy the value system now evolving within me. I kept thinking, 'Why should I work to increase the profits of a corporation? Is this what my life is for?'

One day, Saints with whom I was associating inspired me by saying that there was no shortage of engineers and MBAs in India. There was, however, a need for educated people who could teach spirituality to others. So, with the idea of realizing the Supreme and helping others do the same, I took sanyas.

That was almost 40 years ago. As a monk, I travelled throughout India, associating and learning from elevated saints and residing in many holy places and ashrams. My spiritual quest finally brought me to the lotus feet of Jagadguru Kripaluji Maharaj. Meeting Him was akin to a lost child being united with its mother. I lost my heart to Him from the first moment I saw Him.

Under the tutelage of Shree Maharajji, I extensively studied ancient Vedic texts and the scriptures of other major Eastern and Western religions of the world. Subsequently, Maharajji entrusted me with the key task of sharing the divine knowledge I had received from Him.

I always feel blessed to have the opportunity to lead a life full of meaning, value, and service.

SECRET OF SWAMIJI'S FITNESS

Question: Swamiji, you have a hectic travel schedule and yet stay fit. What is the secret of your fitness?

Answer: My service to God requires me to travel extensively. On average, every year, I visit approximately 70 cities. Within each city, as well, I often stay in a different residence every night. That is why I jokingly tell people that my suitcase travels to 150 homes in a year.

Chanakya's sutras state: 'Intense sunshine reduces the life of clothes. Excessive travel reduces one's lifespan.' So, if I remain in good health, despite all this travel, it is the consequence of the causeless grace of God and Guru. By Their blessings, I am able to do Their work. Without Their mercy, a thousand things could go wrong with my health because the human body is such a complex mechanism.

Nevertheless, to leave it in God's hands would be irresponsible. It would be like saying, 'Let God serve me; I will not do anything.' Instead, from our side as well, we must follow the rules of good health. The scriptures lay special emphasis on maintaining our physical body while engaging in spiritual pursuits. The *Charak*

Samhitā, an Ayurvedic text, states:

śharīra mādhyaṁ khalu dharma sādhanam

'Even for devotion to God, your body is the vehicle, and it must be maintained.'

As for myself, to stay fit, I take a holistic approach—comprising yogasanas, pranayam, and a healthy diet. I target 60 minutes of exercise daily, five to six days a week.

With increasing age, it becomes important to maintain muscle mass. So, I have increased specific postures to do just that. In fact, I have split my yogasana practice into three parts. One day, I focus on the upper body. The next day, I concentrate on the lower body. And the following day, I get cardio through a regimen of Surya Namaskars.

I also enjoy casual walks, as they give an opportunity to unwind and rejuvenate. In each city, devotees join me for morning walks, during which we discuss spiritual topics. It is a great opportunity for them to clarify their doubts in natural settings. Over the years, this has now become a regular tradition at JKYog.

Further, I also eat a balanced diet. Eating healthy is not as complicated as people make it to be. It suffices to follow conventional wisdom and get all nutrients in the right proportions. The idea is to get a good proportion of carbohydrates, fats, vitamins, minerals, and antioxidants. It is also important to stay hydrated. Water helps our body get rid of toxins. You can read more about good eating habits and nutrition in my book, *Science of Healthy Diet*.

Finally, as I travel a lot across cities and villages throughout the year, I must take care of my immunity. For that, I ensure a daily dose of vitamin C through a glass of lemon water. Alternatively, an amla (Indian gooseberry), if it is readily available.

I have combined these components of healthy living into a holistic system called JKYog. It includes five Vedic disciplines for mind management and physical wellness. These are: Radhey Shyam Yogasanas, Radhey Naam Pranayam, Subtle Body Relaxation, Roop Dhyan Meditation, and Science of Proper Diet. You can read more about this holistic system in my book, *Yoga for the Body, Mind and Soul.*

The unique feature of this yogic system is that the practices are blended with devotion. This not only helps to keep the physical body fit but also helps the soul relish the bliss of bhakti. It harmonizes the body, mind, and soul, creating a feeling of well-being from within. We are now offering it under the name 'Prem Yoga'. JKYog also offers International Yoga Alliance-certified 200-hour and 500-hour Yoga Teacher Training courses.

Glossary

abhyās	practice or a concerted and persistent effort to change an old habit or develop a new one
ācharaṇ	implementation
aarti	ceremony of lights, usually performed for deities or the Guru
apauruṣheya	not created by any person
atma	the real self or 'soul' that is spiritual in nature and which imparts consciousness to the body
atma jnana	realized knowledge of the self as the soul
atma samarpan	offering one's soul to God
āyuḥ sattva	foods that promote longevity
bhakti	devotion; love for God
Brahma jnana	realized knowledge of the Supreme
Brahma Muhūrt	also known as Creator's time. Approximately the last two hours of the night immediately preceding sunrise

Braj Ras	bliss of devotion revealed by Shree Krishna in His Pastimes in the land of Braj during His descension 5,000 years ago
chintan	contemplation; to repeatedly revise a piece of knowledge in the intellect
darshan	1) philosophic text written by a sage 2) divine vision
dhams *(dhāms)*	abodes; four holy sites in India
dhan	wealth
diksha *(dīkṣhā)*	initiation ceremony by the Guru; divine power granted by the Guru to the disciple that results in God-realization. Commonly misinterpreted as receiving a mantra in the ear from the Guru
Dwadashi	the day after Ekadashi
Ekadashi	eleventh day of waxing and waning moon
Golok	the divine Abode of Shree Krishna, which exists in the spiritual realm, beyond this material realm
gopis	the village maidens who resided in Braj when Shree Krishna displayed His leelas there 5,000 years ago
gunas	modes of material nature
Guru	a God-realized teacher of spirituality
Iṣhṭa Dev	chosen Form of God that one worships

Itihās	two historical texts of Indian civilization: Ramayan and Mahabharat
japa	chanting of mantra or Name of God, also done wirh rosary beads
jnana	knowledge
jnana abhimān	the 'conceit' of knowledge
jnana-kand (jnana-kāṇḍ)	section of Vedas containing philosophic knowledge
Kali yug	present era on the earth planet. This was preceded by *Dwāpar yug*, *Tretā yug*, and Satya yug
kāraṇ śharīr	causal body consisting of the account of karmas from endless past lives, including the sanskars (tendencies) from previous lives
karm	work in accordance with the prescribed rules of the Vedas
karm kand (karm-kāṇḍ)	1) ritualistic ceremony 2) section of the Vedas dealing with ritualistic ceremonies and duties
karm sanyasi	one who renounces worldly duties and engages only in spiritual practice
karm yog	practice of uniting the mind with God even while doing one's obligatory duties in the world
kirtans	hearing, singing and remembering the Names, Forms, Qualities, Pastimes, Abodes, and Associates of God; usually done in a group

kriyamāṇ karmas	actions we perform in the present life of our free will
leelas	divine Pastimes enacted by God in His personal Form
mana	mind
manan	see *chintan*
mānas rog	mental afflictions. According to the Vedic scriptures, sentiments of anger, jealousy, greed, revenge, desire, pride etc.
manasi seva *(mānasī seva)*	serving God in the mind, by thought
maya baddh	materially bound
maya	the material energy from which this world is created. It also puts souls, who are forgetful of God, into illusion, and makes them transmigrate in the cycle of life and death
*Nibandh*s	philosophical theses by great sages
nididhyāsan	internalize a concept with firm faith
nirguna	not possessing material qualities
nishkaam *(niṣhkām)* bhakti	selfless devotion; worship with the aim of serving God for His happiness alone
nitya leela	eternal Pastimes, generally used in reference to God
pāp purush	sin personified
para *(parā)* bhakti	Divine Love

paaras (pāras)	mythical philosopher's stone
parāyaṇ	recitation of a scripture from beginning to end
pooja	worship
pranayam	practice of breath regulation
pran priyatam	dearer than one's life
prārabdh karmas	the destiny one is allotted at the time of birth, based on past karmas
Prayojak kartā	the one who bestows the power to perform actions e.g. God
prayojya kartā	one who uses the power granted by the *Prayojak kartā*, i.e. individual soul
preya	happiness that seems like ambrosia initially but proves to be poisonous later
Raas leela	the divine dance of Shree Krishna with the gopis of Braj, in which He showered them with the highest bliss of divine love
Radha	God takes on two Forms in His divine Pastimes—Krishna (the Energetic) and Radha (His divine energy). Radha is also called the Divine Mother of the universe, to whom all the other energies of God are subservient.
rāgānugā bhakti	devotion in which the thought of lovingly serving God is all-important
ragas	musical notes

rajas	one of the three modes of material nature; of mode of passion
rasa	sweetness or nectar
Roop Dhyan	a meditation technique propagated by Jagadguru Kripaluji Maharaj in which the meditator sits with eyes closed and focuses on an image or images of any form of God
sadhak (*sādhak*)	spiritual aspirant
sadhan bhakti	preparatory devotion which is done to clean the heart and prepare it for receiving siddha bhakti
sadhana	spiritual practice, usually done daily
sakaam *(sakām)* bhakti	selfishly motivated devotion
samarpan	dedication of oneself or one's works to God
sambandhi	our true and eternal relative, who is God
sañchit karmas	a person's accumulated karmas of endless lifetimes
sanyas	monkhood; renounced order of life
satsang	holy association that takes our mind to the Absolute Truth and purifies our mind
sattva	one of the three modes of material nature; of mode of goodness
seva	to serve
Shad Darshan	six treatises on Indian philosophy
shakti	energy

Shaktiman (Shaktimān)	Energetic; source of energy
Shastras *(Śhāstras)*	scriptures
sharanagat *(śharaṇāgat)*	surrendered soul
sharanagati *(śharaṇāgati)*	surrender of the mind, intellect, and ego to God
shraddha *(śhraddhā)*	faith
shravan (śhravaṇ)	to hear or read divine or spiritual knowledge
śhreya	happiness that appears bitter in the short-term but finally turns into nectar
siddha bhakti	divine love, or perfect devotion, which is a power of God and is received by His grace
smaraṇ	to remember
Smritis	books of dharma
snan *(snān)*	bath
sthūl śharīr	gross body
sthita prajña	sage of steady wisdom
sūkṣhma śharīr	subtle body
tamas	one of the three modes of material nature; of mode of ignorance
tana	body
tapasya	austerity
tota ratat jnana	parrot-like knowledge
triguṇātīt	transcendental to the three modes of material nature
Tulsi	holy basil

upasana kand (upāsanā-kāṇḍ)	section of the Vedas dealing with different kinds of worship
upavās	fast; to not eat or eat and drink selectively for a pre-defined period of time
vaidhi bhakti	devotion in which rituals and ceremonies are emphasized in an attempt to attach the mind to God
vairāgya	detachment from the material world
Vaishnavas	followers of Bhagavan Vishnu
vivek	power of discernment such that the intellect rules the mind
yaksha	semi-celestial beings possessing power and wealth
yog nidra	a meditative yogic practice performed while lying relaxed
yog	from Sanskrit root 'yuj' meaning to join; union of our tiny soul with the Supreme Soul (God)
yogasan	yogic postures
Yogmaya	divine energy of God
yuga dharma	recommended spiritual practice in the present age of Kali

Guide to Hindi Pronunciation

Vowels

अ	*a*	as *u* in 'but'
आ	*ā*	as *a* in 'far'
इ	*i*	as *i* in 'pin'
ई	*ī*	as *i* in 'machine'
उ	*u*	as *u* in 'push'
ऊ	*ū*	as *o* in 'move'
ए	*e*	as *a* in 'evade'
ऐ	*ai*	as *a* in 'mat'; sometimes as *ai* in 'aisle' with the only difference that *a* should be pronounced as *u* in 'but', not as *a* in 'far'
ओ	*o*	as *o* in 'go'
औ	*au*	as *o* in 'pot' or as *aw* in 'saw'
ऋ	*ṛi*	as *ri* in 'Krishna'[6]
ॠ	*ṛī*	as *ree* in 'spree'

[6]Across the many states of India, *ṛi* is pronounced as *ru* as *u* in p*u*sh. In most parts of North India, *ṛi* is pronounced as *ri* in K*ri*shna. We have used the North Indian style here.

Consonants

Gutturals: Pronounced from the throat

क	*ka*	as *k* in 'kite'
ख	*kha*	as *kh* in 'Eckhart'
ग	*ga*	as *g* in 'goat'
घ	*gha*	as *gh* in 'dighard'
ङ	*ṅa*	as *n* in 'finger'

Palatals: Pronounced with the middle of the tongue against the palate

च	*cha*	as *ch* in 'channel'
छ	*chha*	as *chh* in 'staunchheart'
ज	*ja*	as *j* in 'jar'
झ	*jha*	as *dgeh* in 'hedgehog'
ञ	*ña*	as *n* in 'lunch'

Cerebrals: Pronounced with the tip of the tongue against the palate

ट	*ta*	as *t* in 'tub'
ठ	*ṭha*	as *th* in 'hothead'
ड	*ḍa*	as *d* in 'divine'
ढ	*ḍha*	as *dh* in 'redhead'
ण	*ṇa*	as *n* in 'burnt'

Dentals: Pronounced like the cerebrals but with the tongue against the teeth

त	ta	as *t* in the French word 'matron'
थ	tha	as *th* in 'ether'

द	da	as *th* in 'either'
ध	dha	as *dh* in 'Buddha'
न	na	as *n* in 'no'

Labials: Pronounced with the lips

प	*pa*	as *p* in 'pink'
फ	*pha*	as *ph* in 'uphill'
ब	*ba*	as *b* in 'boy'
भ	*bha*	as *bh* in 'abhor'
म	*ma*	as *m* in 'man'

Semivowels

य	*ya*	as *y* in 'yes'
र	*ra*	as *r* in 'remember'
ल	*la*	as *l* in 'light'
व	*va*	as *v* in 'vine', as *w* in 'swan'

Sibilants

श	*śha*	as *sh* in 'shape'
ष	*ṣha*	as *sh* in 'show'
स	*sa*	as *s* in 'sin'

Aspirate

ह	*ha*	as *h* in 'hut'

Visarga

:	*ḥ*	it is a strong aspirate; also lengthens the preceding vowel and occurs only at the end of a word. It is pronounced as a final *h* sound

Anusvara Nasalized

ं	*ṁ/ṅ*	nasalizes and lengthens the preceding vowel and is pronounced as *n* in the words 'and' or 'anthem'[7]
ँ	~	as *n* in 'gung-ho'

Avagraha

ऽ	*Ó*	This is a silent character indicating अ. It is written but not pronounced; used in specific combination (sandhi) rules

Others

क्ष	*kṣha*	as *ksh* in 'freakshow'
ज्ञ	*jña*	as *gy* in 'bigyoung'
ड़	*ṛa*	There is no sign in English to represent the sound ड़. It has been written as *ṛa* but the tip of the tongue quickly flaps down
ढ़	*ṛha*	There is no sign in English to represent the sound ढ़. It has been written as *ṛha* but the tip of the tongue quickly flaps down

[7]Sometimes nasalized and sometimes not. In many words such as *Aṁsh*, *Saṁskar*, etc. are pronounced with a nasal sound as *Aṅsh*, *Saṅskar*, etc. Since it is nasalized, we are using *ṅ*.

Let's Connect

If you enjoyed reading this book and would like to connect with Swami Mukundananda, you can reach him through any of the following channels:

Websites: *www.jkyog.org, www.jkyog.in, www.swamimukundananda.org*

YouTube channels: 'Swami Mukundananda' and 'Swami Mukundananda Hindi'

Facebook: 'Swami Mukundananda' and 'Swami Mukundananda Hindi'

Instagram: 'Swami Mukundananda' and 'Swami Mukundananda Hindi'

Pinterest: Swami Mukundananda – JKYog

Telegram: Swami Mukundananda

Twitter: Swami Mukundananda (@Sw_Mukundananda)

LinkedIn: Swami Mukundananda

Podcasts: Apple, Google, SoundCloud, Spotify, Stitcher

JKYog Radio: TuneIn app for iOS and Android

JKYog App: Available for iOS and Android

WhatsApp Daily Inspirations: We have two broadcast lists. You are welcome to join either or both.

India: +91 84489 41008
USA: +1 346-239-9675

Online Classes:

JKYog India: *www.jkyog.in/online-sessions/*
JKYog US: *www.jkyog.org/online-classes*

Email: deskofswamiji@swamimukundananda.org

To bring *Questions You Always Wanted to Ask* or Swami Mukundananda to your organization—as Google, Intel, Oracle, Verizon, United Nations, Stanford University, Yale University, IITs and IIMs have done—look us up at sm-leadership.org or write to us at info@sm-leadership.org.